QUILTED CRITTERS

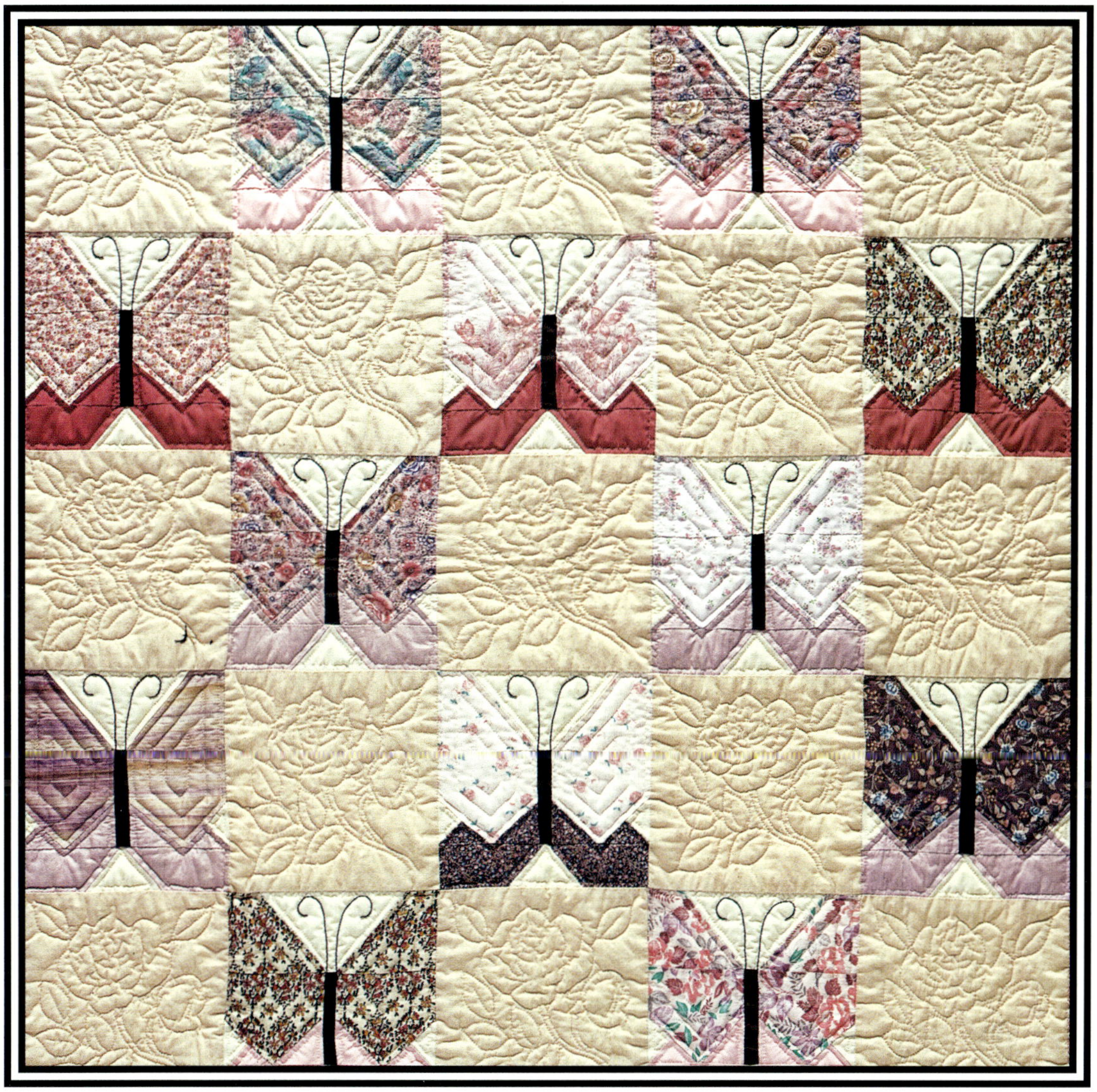

Oxmoor House®

QUILTED CRITTERS

Book Division of Southern Progress Corporation
P.O. Box 2463, Birmingham, AL 35201

Published by Oxmoor House, Inc., and
Leisure Arts, Inc.

Library of Congress Catalog Number: 95-69203
ISBN: 0-8487-1270-6

Manufactured in the United States of America
First Printing 1995

Editor-in-Chief: Nancy Fitzpatrick Wyatt
Editorial Director, Special Interest Publications: Ann H. Harvey
Senior Crafts Editor: Susan Ramey Cleveland
Senior Editor, Editorial Services: Olivia Kindig Wells
Art Director: James Boone

QUILTED CRITTERS

Editor: Janica Lynn York
Copy Editor: Jennifer K. Mathews
Senior Designer: Larry Hunter
Designer: Carol Loria
Illustrator: Kelly Davis
Publishing Systems Administrator: Rick Tucker
Senior Photographer: John O'Hagan
Photo Stylist: Katie Stoddard
Production and Distribution Director: Phillip Lee
Production Manager: Gail H. Morris
Associate Production Manager: Theresa L. Beste
Production Assistant: Marianne Jordan

Contents

Dear Quilting Friends,

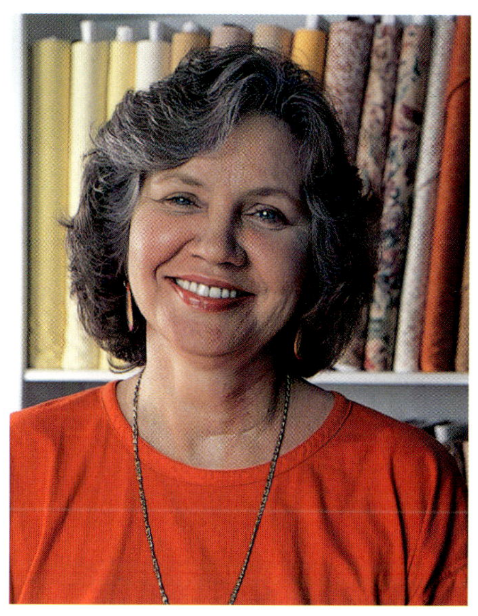

We always had animals when I was growing up—all kinds of animals: parakeets, cats, dogs, rabbits, ducks, turtles, even a horned toad and a chameleon. When I was four or five, Daddy brought home a small billy goat—a very ornery goat with a butting habit. Daddy finally traded that goat for a wind-up record player and a stack of Eddie Arnold records.

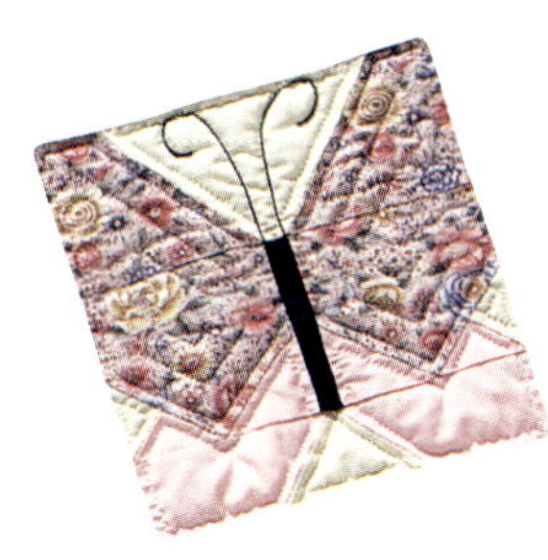

For practical purposes, Mama kept chickens and Daddy raised a few pigs. But my sister and I made animal husbandry a miserable occupation for my parents. Concerned for the chickens' immortal souls, my sister and I one day baptized all the hens and biddies in a washtub in the back yard. Most of them survived the experience. Each fall, when hog-killing time arrived, we put up an awful ruckus at the idea of anyone slaughtering the animals that we had named and thought of as pets, if not family members. To this day, my sister won't eat pork.

Perhaps the ten quilts in this book will remind you of animal friends from your childhood. If not, I hope they'll at least inspire you to pick up your needle and start stitching. Here is a veritable animal kingdom of quilts—from Marta Amundson's *When Pigs Have Wings* on page 15 to *Buttonhole Butterflies* on page 30, made by Ramey Channell (that sister who helped me baptize the chickens). You'll find *Bunnies in the Garden* on page 40 and a *Cow in the Clover* on page 37—both from the Vanessa-Ann Collection. There are pecking hens, kissing dinosaurs, and swimming turtles. Find your favorite critter and quilt up some fun.

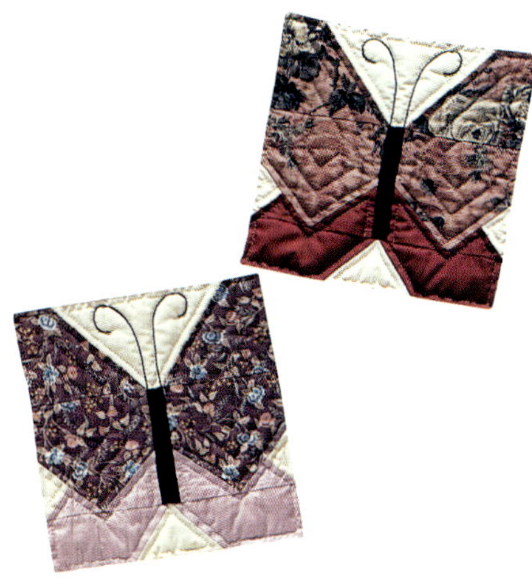

Happy stitching,

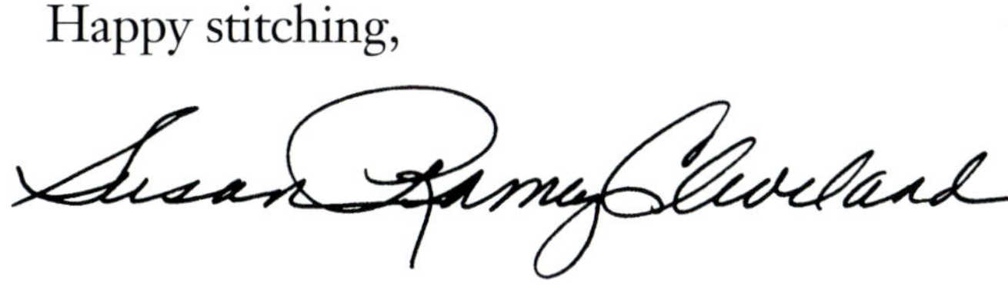

WORKSHOP

Selecting Fabrics

The best fabric for quilts is 100% cotton. Yardage requirements are based on 44"-wide fabric and allow for shrinkage. All fabrics, including backing, should be machine-washed, dried, and pressed before cutting. Use warm water and detergent but not fabric softener.

Necessary Notions

- Scissors
- Rotary cutter and mat
- Acrylic rulers
- Template plastic
- Pencils for marking cutting lines
- Sewing needles
- Sewing thread
- Sewing machine
- Seam ripper
- Pins
- Iron and ironing board
- Quilting needles
- Thimble
- Hand quilting thread
- Machine quilting thread

Making Templates

A template is a duplication of a printed pattern, made from a sturdy material, which is traced onto fabric. Many regular shapes such as squares and triangles can be marked directly on the fabric with a ruler, but you need templates for other shapes. Some quiltmakers use templates for all shapes.

You can trace patterns directly onto template plastic. Or make a template by tracing a pattern onto graph paper and gluing the paper to posterboard or sandpaper. (Sandpaper will not slip on fabric.)

When a large pattern is given in two pieces, make one template for the complete piece.

Cut out the template on the marked line. It is important that a template be traced, marked, and cut accurately. If desired, punch out corner dots with a ⅛"-diameter hole punch **(Diagram 1).**

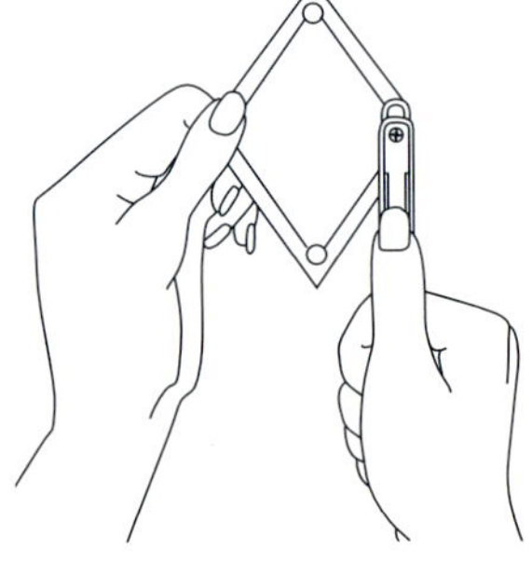

Diagram 1

Mark each template with its letter and grain line. Verify the template's accuracy, placing it over the printed pattern. Any discrepancy, however small, is multiplied many times as the quilt is assembled. Another way to check templates' accuracy is to make a test block before cutting more pieces.

Tracing Templates on Fabric

For hand piecing, templates should be cut to the finished size of the piece so seam lines can be marked on the fabric. Avoiding the selvage, place the template *facedown* on the *wrong* side of the fabric, aligning the template grain line with the straight grain. Hold the template firmly and trace around it. Repeat as needed, leaving ½" between tracings **(Diagram 2).**

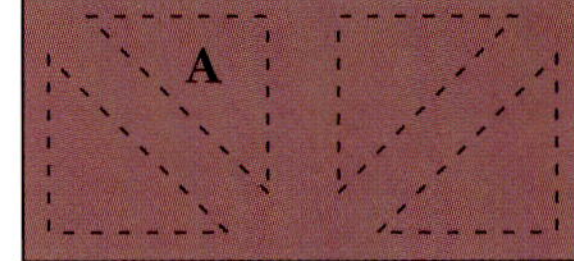

Diagram 2

For machine piecing, templates should include seam allowances. These templates are used in the same manner as for hand piecing, but you can mark the fabric using common lines for efficient cutting **(Diagram 3).** Mark corners on fabric through holes in the template.

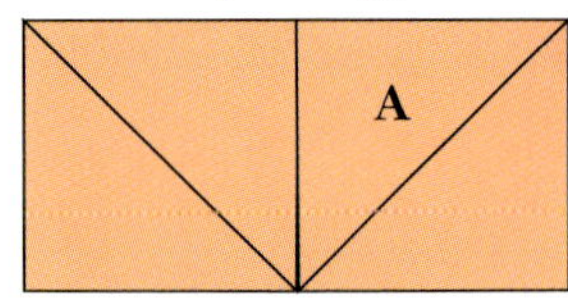

Diagram 3

For hand or machine piecing, use window templates to enhance accuracy by drawing and cutting out both cutting and sewing lines. The guidance of a drawn seam line is very useful for sewing set-in seams, when pivoting at a precise point is critical. Used on the right side of the fabric, window templates help you cut specific motifs with accuracy **(Diagram 4).**

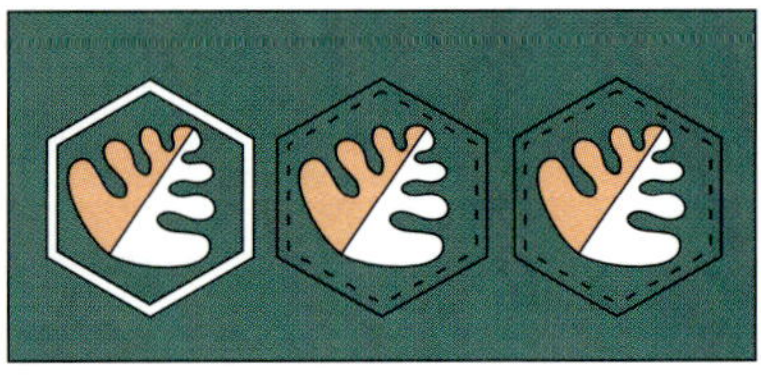

Diagram 4

For hand appliqué, templates should be made the finished size. Place templates *faceup* on the *right* side of the fabric. Position tracings at least ½" apart **(Diagram 5).** Add a ¼" seam allowance around pieces when cutting.

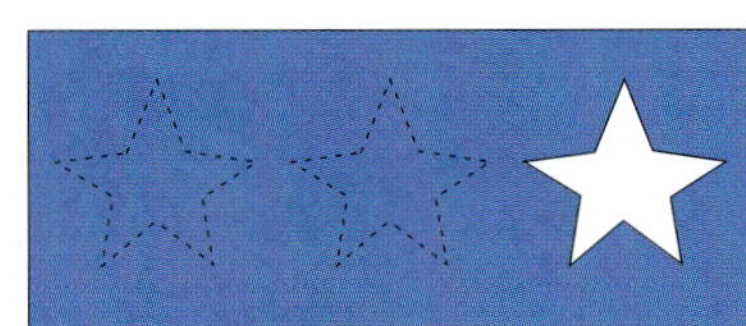

Diagram 5

Cutting

Grain Lines

Woven threads form the fabric's grain. Lengthwise grain, parallel to the selvages, has the least stretch; crosswise grain has a little more give.

Long strips such as borders should be cut lengthwise whenever possible and cut first to ensure that you have the necessary length. Usually, other pieces can be cut aligned with either grain.

Bias is the 45° diagonal line between the two grain directions. Bias has the most stretch and is used for curving strips such as flower stems. Bias is often preferred for binding.

Never use the selvage (finished edge). Selvage does not react to washing, drying, and pressing like the rest of the fabric and may pucker when the finished quilt is laundered.

Rotary Cutting

A rotary cutter, used with a protective mat and a ruler, takes getting used to but is very efficient for cutting strips, squares, and triangles. A rotary cutter is fast because you can measure and cut multiple layers with a single stroke, without templates or marking. It is also more accurate than cutting with scissors because fabrics remain flat and do not move during cutting.

Because the blade is very sharp, be sure to get a rotary cutter with a safety guard. Keep the guard in the safe position at all times, except when making a cut. *Always keep the cutter out of the reach of children.*

Use the cutter with a self-healing mat. A good mat for cutting strips is at least 23" wide.

1. Squaring the fabric is the first step in accurate cutting. Fold the fabric with selvages aligned. With the yardage to your right, align a small square ruler with the fold near the cut edge. Place a long ruler against the left side of the square **(Diagram 6).** Keeping the long ruler in place, remove the square. Hold the ruler in place with your left hand as you cut, rolling the cutter *away from you* along the ruler's edge with a steady motion. You can move your left hand along the ruler as you cut, but do not change the position of the ruler. *Keep your fingers away from the ruler's edge when cutting.*

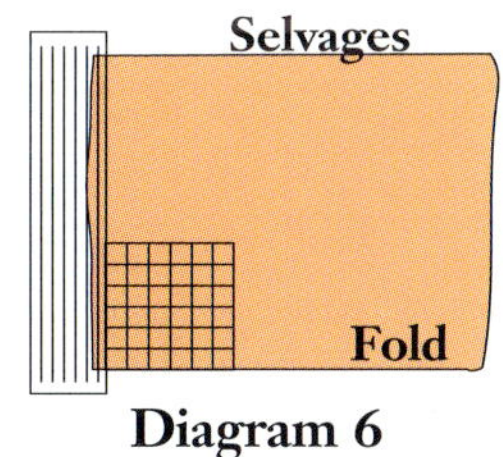

Diagram 6

2. Open the fabric. If the cut was not accurately perpendicular to the fold, the edge will be V-shaped instead of straight **(Diagram 7).** Correct the cut if necessary.

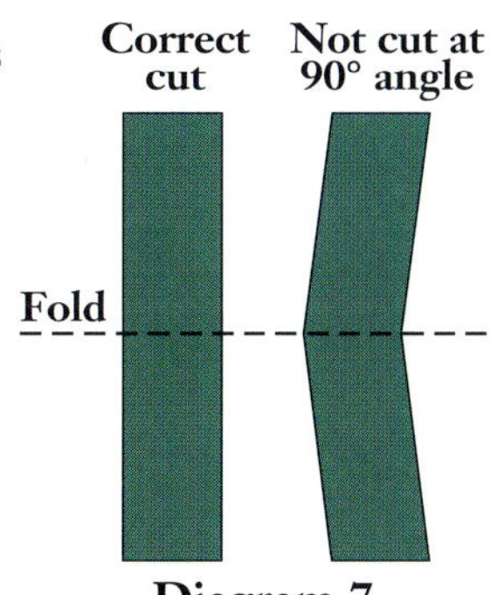

Diagram 7

3. With a transparent ruler, you can measure and cut at the same time. Fold the fabric in half again, aligning the selvages with the fold, making four layers that line up perfectly along the cut edge. Project instructions designate the strip width needed. Position the ruler to measure the correct distance from the edge **(Diagram 8)** and cut. The blade will easily cut through all four layers. Check the strip to be sure the cut is straight. The strip length is the width of the fabric, approximately 43" to 44". Using the ruler again, trim selvages, cutting about ⅜" from each end.

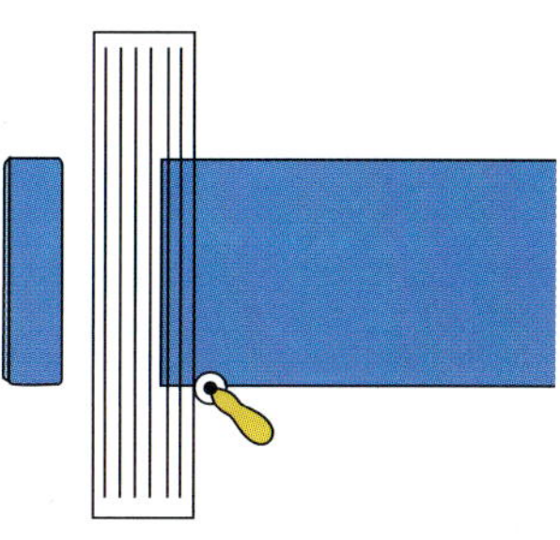

Diagram 8

4. To cut squares and rectangles from a strip, align the desired measurement on the ruler with the strip end and cut across the strip **(Diagram 9).**

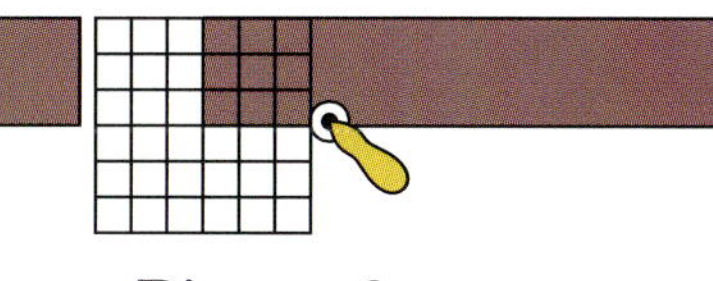

Diagram 9

5. Cut triangles from squares or rectangles. Cutting instructions often direct you to cut a square in half or in quarters diagonally to make right triangles, and this technique can apply to rectangles, too **(Diagram 10).** The outside edges of the square or rectangle are on the straight of the grain, so triangle sides cut on the diagonal are bias.

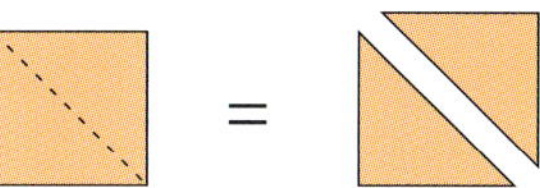

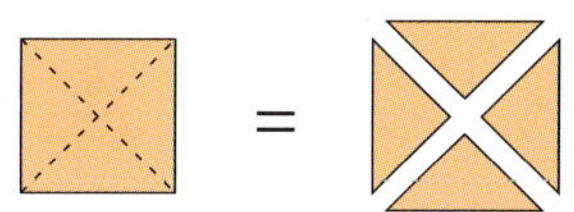

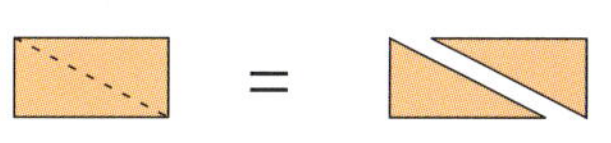

6. Some projects in this book use a time-saving technique called strip piecing. With this method, strips are joined to make a pieced band. Cut across the seams of this band to cut preassembled units **(Diagram 11).**

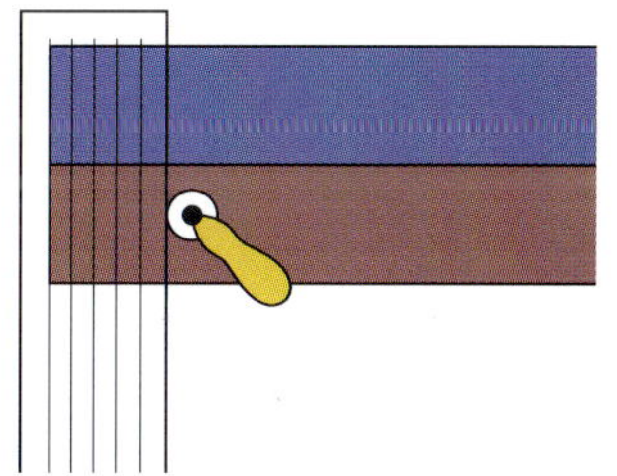

Diagram 11

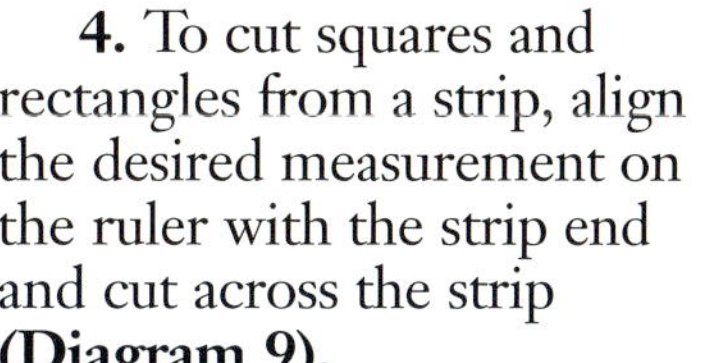

Machine Piecing

Your sewing machine does not have to be a new, computerized model. A good straight stitch is all that's necessary, but it may be helpful to have a nice satin stitch for appliqué. Clean and oil your machine regularly, use good-quality thread, and replace needles frequently.

1. Patches for machine piecing are cut with the seam allowance included, but the sewing line is not usually marked. Therefore, a way to make a consistent ¼" seam is essential. Some presser feet have a right toe that is ¼" from the needle. Other machines have an adjustable needle that can be set for a ¼" seam. If your machine has neither feature, experiment to find how the fabric must be placed to make a ¼" seam. Mark this position on the presser foot or throat plate.

2. Use a stitch length that makes a strong seam but is not too difficult to remove with a seam ripper. The best setting is usually 10 to 12 stitches per inch.

3. Pin only when really necessary. If a straight seam is less than 4" and does not have to match an adjoining seam, pinning is not necessary.

4. When intersecting seams must align **(Diagram 12),** match the units with right sides facing and push a pin through both seams at the seam line. Turn the pinned unit to the right side to check the alignment; then pin securely. As you sew, remove each pin just before the needle reaches it.

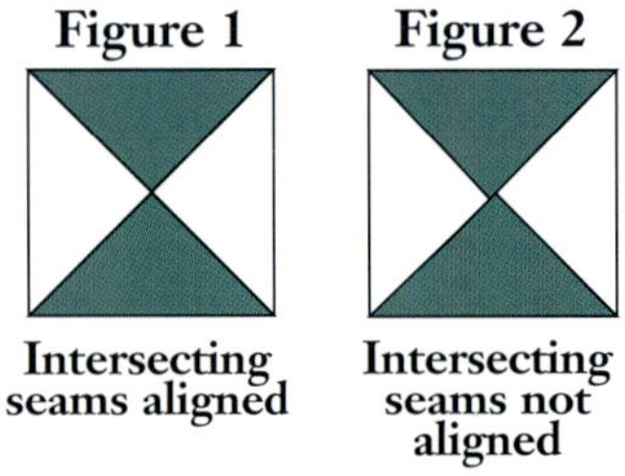

Figure 1 — Intersecting seams aligned

Figure 2 — Intersecting seams not aligned

Diagram 12

5. Block assembly diagrams are used throughout this book to show how pieces should be joined. Make small units first; then join them in rows and continue joining rows to finish the block **(Diagram 13).** Blocks are joined in the same manner to complete the quilt top.

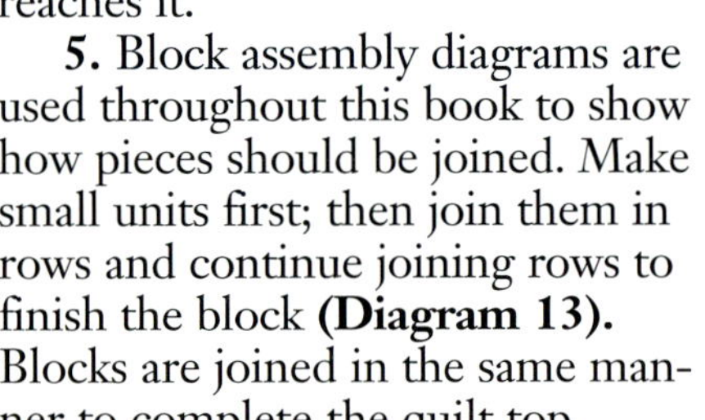

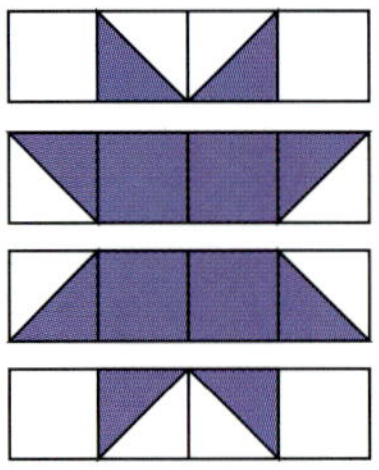

Diagram 13

6. Chain piecing saves time. Stack pieces to be sewn in pairs, with right sides facing. Join the first pair as usual. At the end of the seam, do not backstitch, cut the thread, or lift the presser foot. Just feed in the next pair of pieces—the machine will make a few stitches between pieces before the needle strikes the second piece of fabric. Continue sewing in this way until all pairs are joined. Stack the chain of pieces until you are ready to clip them apart **(Diagram 14).**

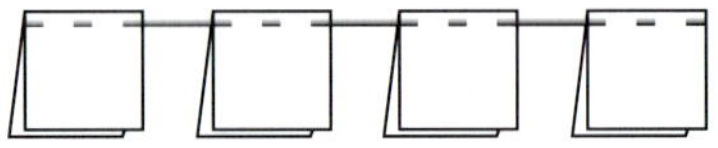

Diagram 14

7. Most seams are sewn straight across, from raw edge to raw edge. Since they will be crossed by other seams, they do not require backstitching to secure them.

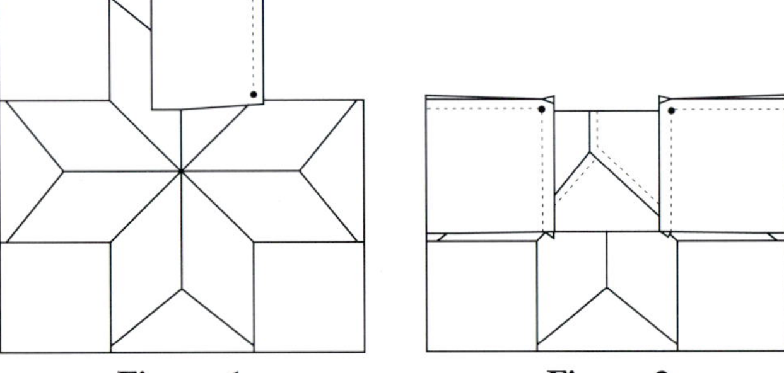

Figure 1 **Figure 2**

Diagram 15

8. When piecing diamonds or other angled seams, you may need to make set-in seams. For these, always mark the corner dots (shown on the patterns) on the fabric pieces. Stitch one side, starting at the outside edge and being careful not to sew beyond the dot into the seam allowance **(Diagram 15, Figure A).** Backstitch. Align the other side of the piece as needed, with right sides facing. Sew from the dot to the outside edge **(Figure B).**

9. Sewing curved seams requires extra care. First, mark the centers of both the convex (outward) and concave (inward) curves **(Diagram 16).** Staystitch just inside the seam allowance of both pieces. Clip the concave piece to the stitching **(Figure A).** With right sides facing and raw edges aligned, pin the two patches together at the center **(Figure B)** and at the left edge **(Figure C).** Sew from edge to center, stopping frequently to check that the raw edges are aligned. Stop at the center with the needle down. Raise the presser foot and pin the pieces together from the center to the right edge. Lower the foot and continue to sew. Press seam allowances toward the concave curve **(Figure D).**

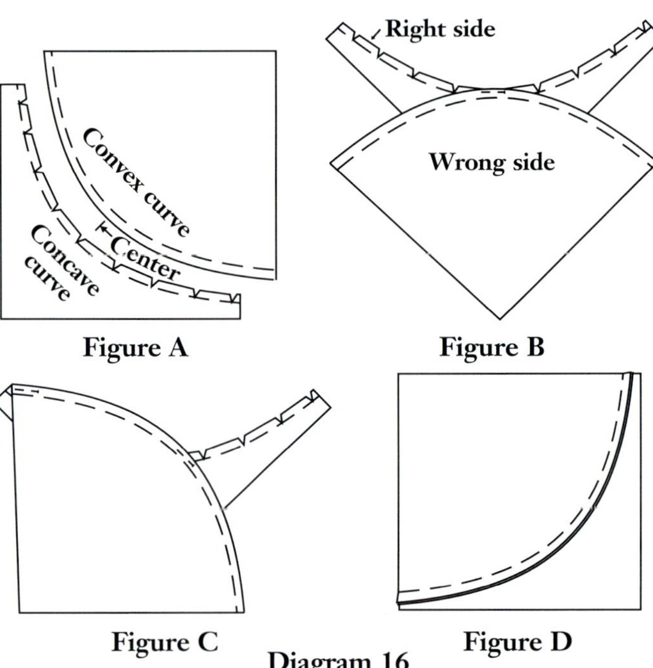

Figure A **Figure B**

Figure C **Figure D**

Diagram 16

Hand Piecing

Make a running stitch of 8 to 10 stitches per inch along the marked seam line on the wrong side of the fabric. Don't pull the fabric as you sew; let the pieces lie relaxed in your hand. Sew from seam line to seam line, not from edge to edge as in machine piecing.

When ending a line of stitching, backstitch over the last stitch and make a loop knot **(Diagram 17).**

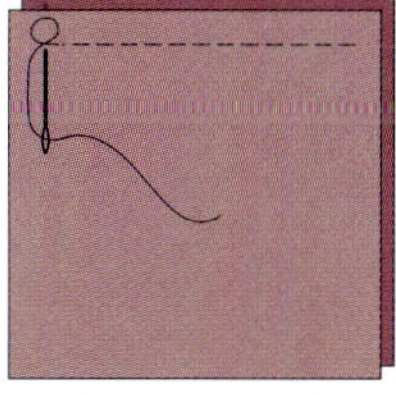

Diagram 17

Match seams and points accurately, pinning patches together before piecing. Align match points as described in Step 4 under Machine Piecing.

When joining units where several seams meet, do not sew over seam allowances; sew *through* them at the match point **(Diagram 18).** When four or more seams meet, press the seam allowances in the same direction to reduce bulk **(Diagram 19).**

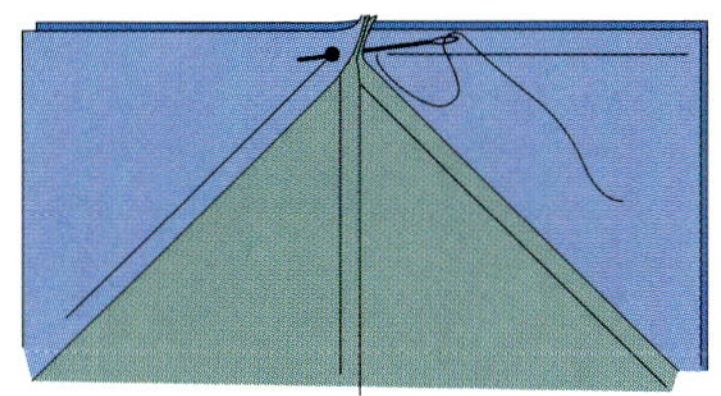

Diagram 18

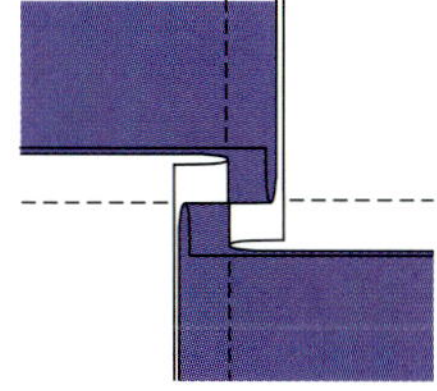

Diagram 19

Pressing

Careful pressing is necessary for precise piecing. Press each seam as you go. Sliding the iron back and forth may push the seam out of shape. Use an up-and-down motion, lifting the iron from spot to spot. Press the seam flat on the wrong side. Open the piece and, on the right side, press both seam allowances to one side (usually toward the darker fabric). Pressing the seam open leaves tiny gaps through which batting may beard.

Appliqué

Traditional Hand Appliqué

Hand appliqué requires that you turn under a seam allowance around the shape to prevent frayed edges.

1. Trace around the template on the right side of the fabric. This line indicates where to turn the seam allowance. Cut each piece approximately ¼" outside the line.

2. For simple shapes, turn the edges by pressing the seam allowance to the back; complex shapes may require basting the seam allowance. Sharp points and strong curves are best appliquéd with freezer paper. Clip curves to make a smooth edge. With practice, you can work without pressing seam allowances, turning edges under with the needle as you sew.

3. Do not turn under any seam allowance that will be covered by another appliqué piece.

4. To stitch, use one strand of cotton-wrapped polyester sewing thread in a color that matches the appliqué. Use a slipstitch, but keep the stitch very small on the surface. Working from right to left (or left to right if you're left-handed), pull the needle through the base fabric and catch only a few threads on the folded edge of the appliqué. Reinsert the needle into the base fabric, under the top thread on the appliqué edge to keep the thread from tangling **(Diagram 20).**

5. An alternative to slipstitching is to work a decorative buttonhole stitch around each figure **(Diagram 21).**

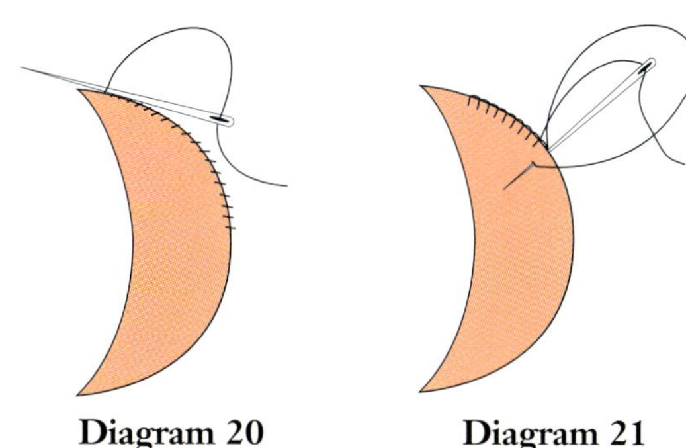

Diagram 20 **Diagram 21**

Freezer Paper Hand Appliqué

Supermarket freezer paper saves time because it eliminates the need for basting seam allowances.

1. Trace the template onto the *dull* side of the freezer paper and cut the paper on the marked line. *Note:* If a design is not symmetrical, turn the template over and trace a mirror image so the fabric piece won't be reversed when you cut it out.

2. Pin the freezer-paper shape, with its *shiny side* up, to the *wrong side* of the fabric. Following the paper shape and adding a scant ¼" seam allowance, cut out the fabric piece. Do not remove pins.

3. Using just the tip of a dry iron, press the seam allowance to the shiny side of the paper. Be careful not to touch the freezer paper with the iron.

4. Appliqué the piece to the background as in traditional appliqué. Trim the fabric from behind the shape, leaving ¼" seam allowances. Separate the freezer paper from the fabric with your fingernail and pull gently to remove it. If you prefer not to trim the background fabric, pull out the freezer paper before you complete stitching.

5. Sharp points require special attention. Turn the point down and press it **(Diagram 22, Figure A).** Fold the seam allowance on one side over the point and press **(Figure B);** then fold the other seam allowance over the point and press **(Figure C).**

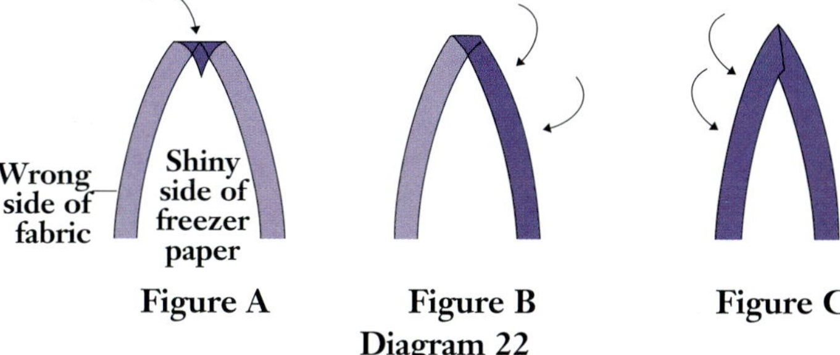

Figure A **Figure B** **Figure C**

Diagram 22

6. When pressing curved edges, clip sharp inward curves **(Diagram 23).** If the shape doesn't curve smoothly, separate the paper from the fabric with your fingernail and try again.

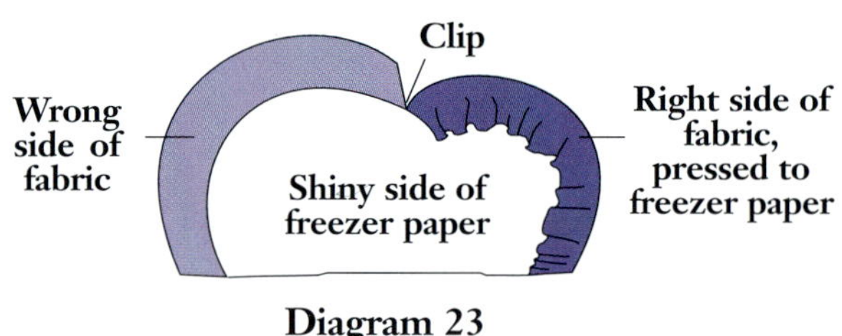

Diagram 23

7. Remove the pins when all seam allowances have been pressed to the freezer paper. Position the prepared appliqué right side up on the background fabric. Press to adhere it to the background fabric.

Machine Appliqué

A machine-sewn satin stitch makes a neat edging. For machine appliqué, cut appliqué pieces without adding seam allowances.

Using fusible web to adhere pieces to the background adds a stiff extra layer to the appliqué and is not appropriate for some quilts. It is best used on small pieces, difficult fabrics, or for wall hangings and accessories in which added stiffness is acceptable. The web prevents fraying and shifting during appliqué.

Place tear-away stabilizer under the background fabric behind the appliqué. Machine-stitch the appliqué edges with a satin stitch or close-spaced zigzag **(Diagram 24).** Test the stitch length and width on a sample first. Use an open-toed presser foot. Remove the stabilizer when appliqué is complete.

Diagram 24

Measuring Borders

Because seams may vary and fabrics may stretch a bit, opposite sides of your assembled quilt top may not be the same measurement. You can (and should) correct this when you add borders.

Measure the length of each side of the quilt. Trim the side border strips to match the *shorter* of the two sides. Join borders to the quilt as described below, easing the longer side of the quilt to fit the border. Join borders to the top and bottom edges in the same manner.

Straight Borders

Side borders are usually added first **(Diagram 25).** With right sides facing and raw edges aligned, pin the center of one border strip to the center of one side of the quilt top. Pin the border to the quilt at each end and then pin along the side as desired. Machine-stitch with the border strip on top. Press the seam allowance toward the border. Trim excess border fabric at each end. In the same manner, add the border to the opposite side and then the top and bottom borders **(Diagram 26).**

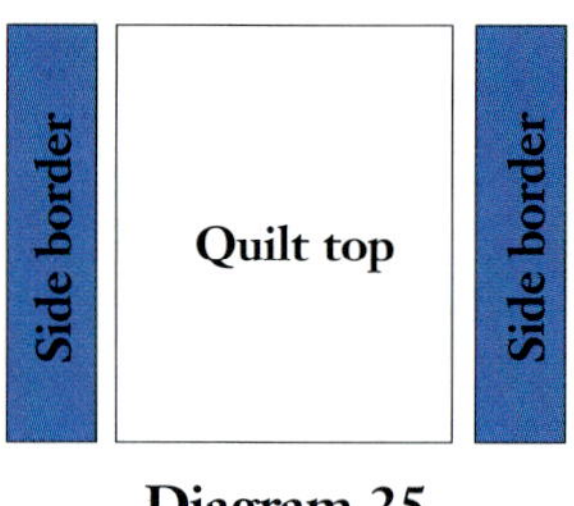

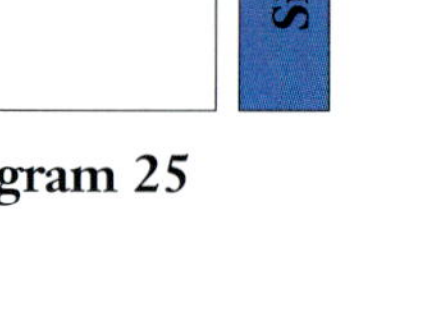
Diagram 25

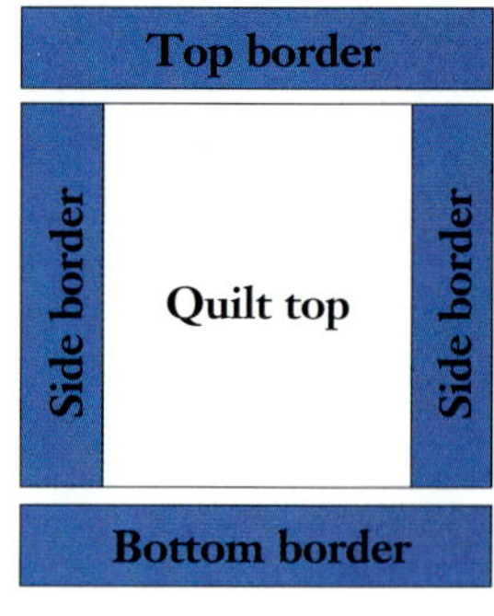

Diagram 26

Mitered Borders

1. Measure your quilt sides. Trim the side border strips to fit the shorter side *plus* the width of the border *plus* 2".

2. Center the measurement of the shorter side on one border strip, placing a pin at each end and at the center of the measurement.

3. With right sides facing and raw edges aligned, match the pins on the border strip to the center and corners of the longer side of the quilt. (Border fabric will extend beyond the corners.)

4. Start machine-stitching at the top pin, backstitching to lock the stitches. Continue to sew, easing the quilt between pins. Stop at the last pin and backstitch. Join remaining borders in the same manner. Press seam allowances toward borders.

5. With right sides facing, fold the quilt diagonally, aligning the raw edges of adjacent borders. Pin securely **(Diagram 27).**

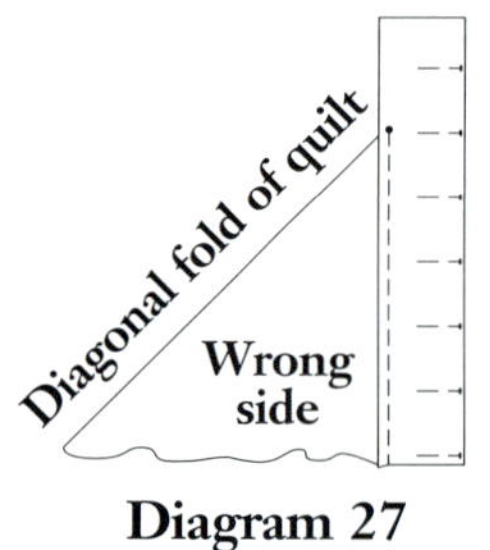

Diagram 27

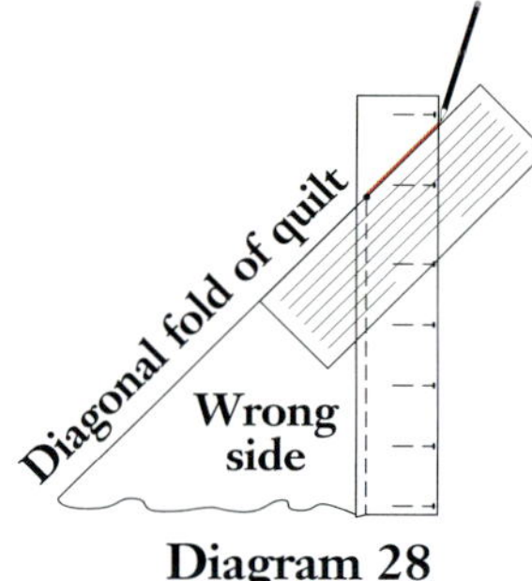

Diagram 28

6. Align a yardstick or quilter's ruler along the diagonal fold **(Diagram 28).** Holding the ruler firmly, mark a line from the end of the border seam to the raw edge.

7. Start machine-stitching at the beginning of the marked line, backstitch, and then stitch on the line out to the raw edge.

8. Unfold the quilt to be sure that the corner lies flat. Correct the stitching if necessary. Trim the seam allowance to ¼".

9. Miter the remaining corners in the same manner. Press the corner seams open.

Quilting Without Marking

Some quilts can be quilted in-the-ditch (right along the seam line), outline-quilted (¼" from the seam line), or echo-quilted (lines of quilting rippling outward from the design like waves on a pond). These methods can be used without any marking at all. If you are machine quilting, simply use the edge of your presser foot and the seam line as a guide. If you are hand quilting, by the time you have pieced a quilt top, your eye will be practiced enough for you to produce straight, even quilting without the guidance of marked lines.

Marking Quilting Designs

Many quilters like to mark the entire top at one time, a practice that requires long-lasting markings. The most common tool for this purpose is a sharp **pencil.** However, most pencils are made with an oil-based graphite lead, which often will not wash out completely. Look for a high-quality artist's pencil marked "2H" or higher (the higher the number, the harder the lead, and the lighter the line it will make). Sharpen the pencil frequently to keep the line on the fabric thin and light. Or try a mechanical pencil with a 0.5-mm lead. It will maintain a fine line without sharpening.

While you are in the art supply store, get a **white plastic eraser** (brand name Magic Rub). This eraser, used by professional drafters and artists, will cleanly remove the carbon smudges left by pencil lead without fraying the fabric or leaving eraser crumbs.

Water- and **air-soluble marking pens** are convenient, but controversial, marking tools. Some quilters have found that the marks reappear, often up to several years later, while others have no problems with them.

Be sure to test these pens on each fabric you plan to mark and *follow package directions exactly.* Because the inks can be permanently set by heat, be very careful with a marked quilt. Do not leave it in your car on a hot day and never touch it with an iron until the marks have been removed. Plan to complete the quilting within a year after marking it with a water-soluble pen.

Air-soluble pens are best for marking small sections at a time. The marks disappear within 24 to 48 hours, but the ink remains in the fabric until it is washed. After the quilt is completed and before it is used, rinse it twice in clear, cool water, using no soap, detergent, or bleach. Let the quilt air-dry.

For dark fabrics, the cleanest marker you can use is a thin sliver of pure, white **soap.** Choose a soap that contains no creams, deodorants, dyes, or perfumes; these added ingredients may leave a residue on the fabric.

Other marking tools include **colored pencils** made specifically for marking fabric and **tailor's chalk** (available in powdered, stick, and traditional cake form). When using chalk, mark small sections of the quilt at a time because the chalk rubs off easily.

Quilting Stencils

Quilting patterns can be purchased as precut stencils. Simply lay these on your quilt top and mark the design through the cutout areas.

To make your own stencil of a printed quilting pattern, such as the one below, use a permanent marker to trace the design onto a blank sheet of template plastic. Then use a craft knife to cut out the design.

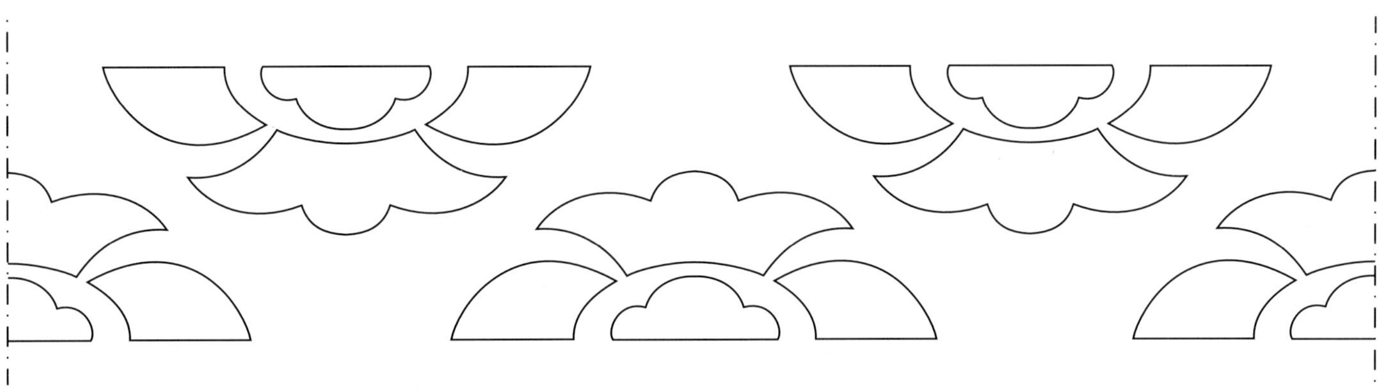

Quilting Stencil Pattern

Making a Quilt Backing

Some fabric and quilt shops sell 90" and 108" widths of 100% cotton fabric that are very practical for quilt backing. However, the instructions in this book always give backing yardage based on 44"-wide fabric.

When using 44"-wide fabric, all quilts wider than 41" will require a pieced backing. For quilts 41" to 80" wide, you will need an amount of fabric equal to two times the desired *length* of the unfinished backing. (The unfinished backing should be at least 3" larger on all sides than the quilt top.)

The simplest method of making a backing is to cut the fabric in half widthwise **(Diagram 29),** and then sew the two panels together lengthwise. This results in a backing with a vertical center seam. Press the seam allowances to one side.

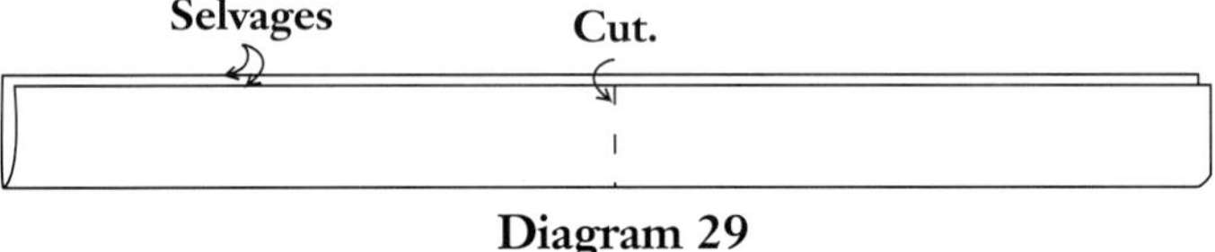

Diagram 29

Another method of seaming the backing results in two vertical seams and a center panel of fabric. This method is often preferred by quilt show judges. Begin by cutting the fabric in half widthwise. Open the two lengths and stack them, with right sides facing and selvages aligned. Stitch along *both* selvage edges to create a tube of fabric **(Diagram 30).** Cut down the center of the top layer of fabric only and open the fabric flat **(Diagram 31).** Press seam allowances to one side.

Diagram 30

If the quilt is wider than 80", it is more economical to cut the fabric into three lengths that are the desired width of the backing. Join the three lengths so that the seams are horizontal to the quilt, rather than vertical. For this method, you'll need an amount of fabric equal to three times the *width* of the unfinished backing.

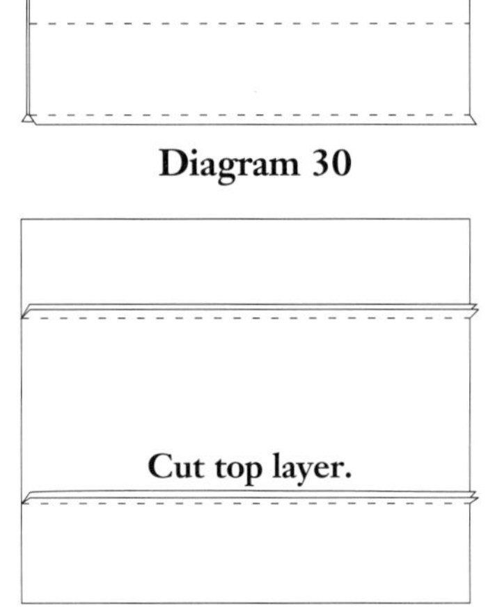

Diagram 31

Fabric requirements in this book reflect the most economical method of seaming the backing fabric.

Layering and Basting

After the quilt top and backing are made, the next steps are layering and basting in preparation for quilting.

Prepare a large working surface to spread out the quilt—a large table, two tables pushed together, or the floor. Place the backing on the working surface wrong side up. Unfold the batting and place it on top of the backing, smoothing away any wrinkles or lumps.

Lay the quilt top wrong side down on top of the batting and backing. Make sure the edges of the backing and quilt top are parallel.

Knot a long strand of sewing thread and use a long (darning) needle for basting. Begin basting in the center of the quilt and baste out toward the edges. The basting stitches should cover an ample amount of the quilt so that the layers do not shift during quilting.

Machine quilters use nickel-plated safety pins for basting so there will be no basting threads to get caught on the presser foot. Safety pins, spaced approximately 4" apart, can be used by hand quilters, too.

Hand Quilting

Hand-quilted stitches should be evenly spaced, with the spaces between stitches about the same length as the stitches themselves. The *number* of stitches per inch is less important than the *uniformity* of the stitching. Don't worry if you take only five or six stitches per inch; just be consistent throughout the project.

Machine Quilting

For machine quilting, the backing and batting should be 3" larger all around than the quilt top, because the quilting process pushes the quilt top fabric outward. After quilting, trim the backing and batting to the same size as the quilt top.

Thread your bobbin with good-quality sewing thread (not quilting thread) in a color to match the backing. Use a top thread color to match the quilt top or use invisible nylon thread.

An even-feed or walking foot will feed all the quilt's layers through the machine at the same speed. It is possible to machine-quilt without this foot (by experimenting with tension and presser foot pressure), but it will be much easier *with* it. If you do not have this foot, get one from your sewing machine dealer.

Straight-Grain Binding

1. Mark the fabric in horizontal lines the width of the binding **(Diagram 32).**

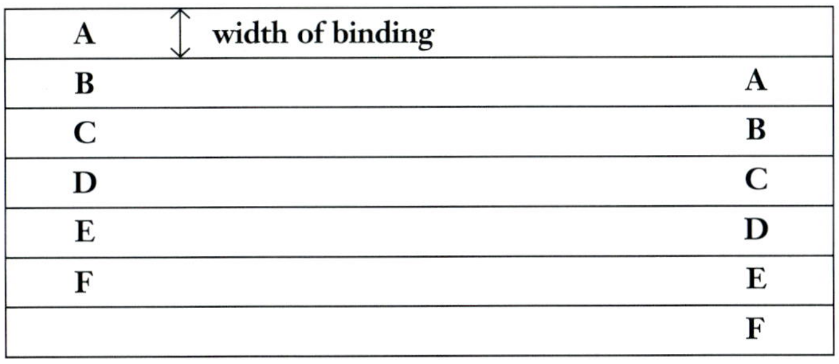

A ↕ width of binding	
B	A
C	B
D	C
E	D
F	E
	F

Diagram 32

2. With right sides facing, fold the fabric in half, offsetting drawn lines by matching letters and raw edges **(Diagram 33).** Stitch a ¼" seam.

3. Cut the binding in a continuous strip, starting with one end and following the marked lines around the tube. Press the strip in half lengthwise.

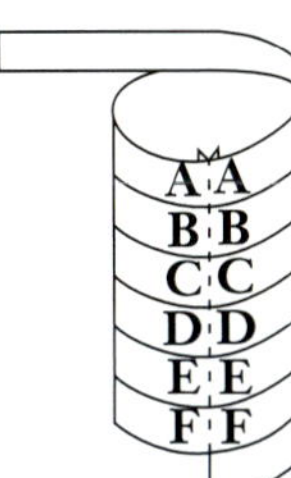

Diagram 33

Continuous Bias Binding

This technique can be used to make continuous bias for appliqué as well as for binding.

1. Cut a square of fabric in half diagonally to form two triangles. With right sides facing, join the triangles **(Diagram 34).** Press the seam allowance open.

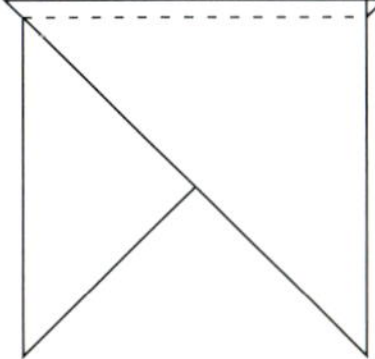

Diagram 34

2. Mark parallel lines the desired width of the binding **(Diagram 35),** taking care not to stretch the bias. With right sides facing, align the raw edges (indicated as Seam 2). As you align the edges, offset one Seam 2 point past its natural matching point by one line. Stitch the seam; then press the seam allowance open.

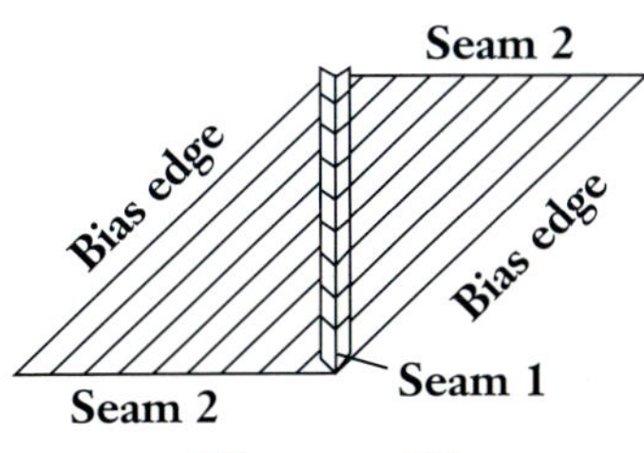

Diagram 35

3. Cut the binding in a continuous strip, starting with the protruding point and following the marked lines around the tube **(Diagram 36).** Press the strip in half lengthwise.

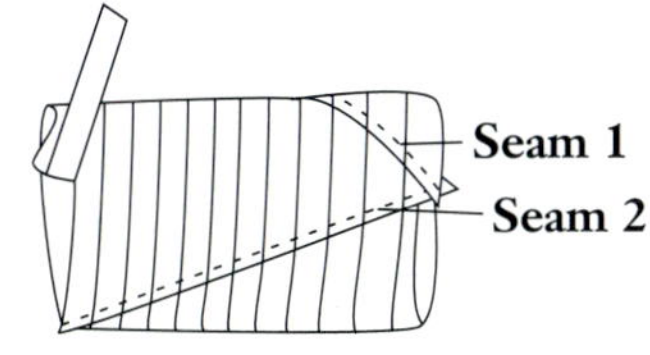

Diagram 36

Applying Binding

Binding is applied to the front of the quilt first. You may begin anywhere on the edge of the quilt except at the corner.

1. Matching raw edges, lay the binding on the quilt. Fold down the top corner of the binding at a 45° angle, align the raw edges, and pin **(Diagram 37).**

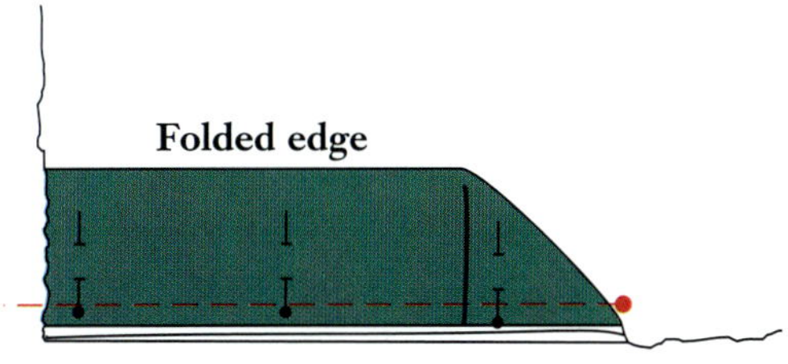

Diagram 37

2. Beginning at the folded end, machine-stitch the binding to the quilt. Stop stitching ¼" from the corner and backstitch. Fold the binding strip diagonally away from the quilt, making a 45° angle **(Diagram 38).**

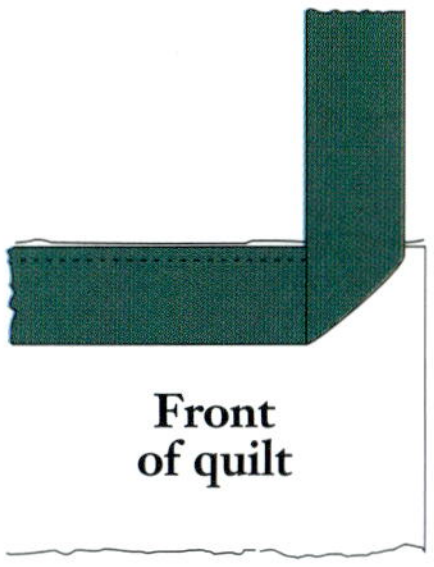

Front of quilt

Diagram 38

3. Fold the binding strip straight down along the next side to be stitched, creating a pleat in the corner. Position the needle at the ¼" seam line of the new side **(Diagram 39).** Make a few stitches, backstitch, and then stitch the seam. Continue until all corners and sides are done. Overlap the end of the binding strip over the beginning fold and stitch about 2" beyond it. Trim any excess binding.

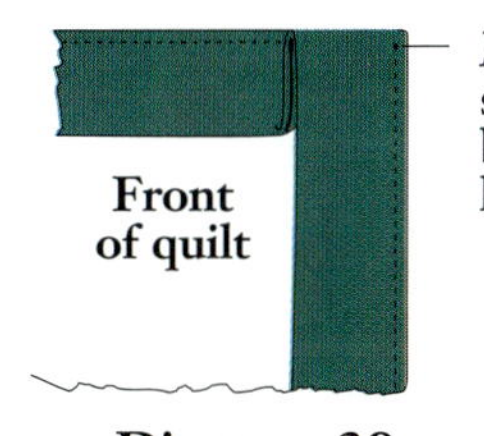

Diagram 39

4. Turn the binding over the raw edge of the quilt. Slipstitch it in place on the back, using thread that matches the binding. The fold at the beginning of the binding strip will create a neat, angled edge when it is folded to the back.

5. At each corner, fold the binding to form a miter **(Diagram 40).** Hand-stitch the miters closed if desired.

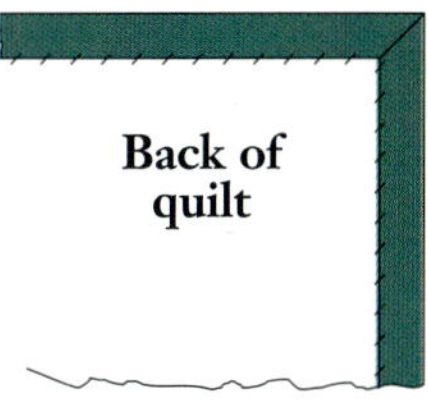

Diagram 40

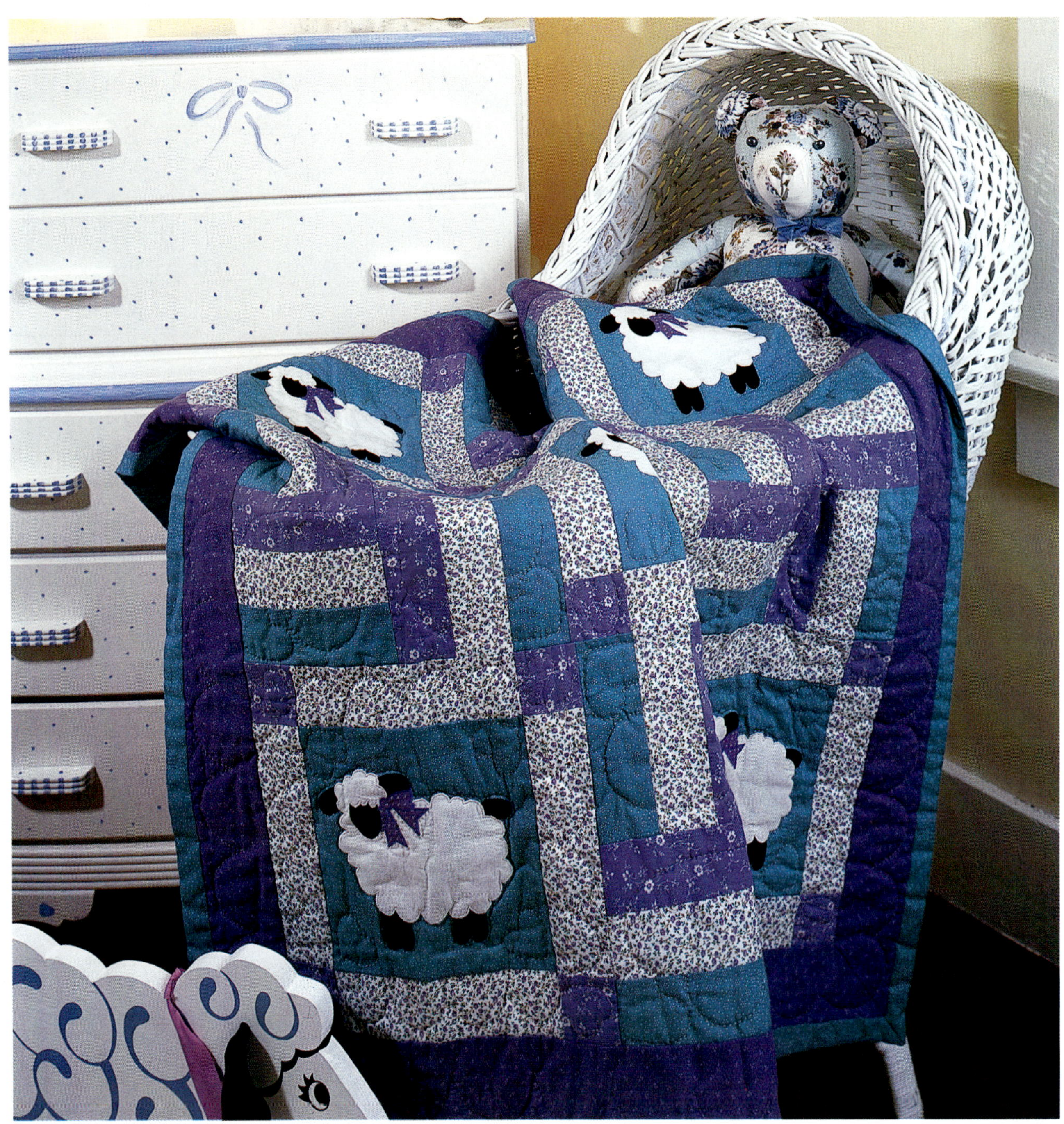

Quilt by Louisa Wilson
Cadyville, New York

Sheep and Rail Fence

Louisa Wilson has been sewing ever since her mother taught her how to make clothes for her dolls. "I soon discovered the joy of coordinating fabrics and designing things myself," says Louisa. "I like to take a traditional quilt block and design an appliqué to go with it, as in *Sheep and Rail Fence.*"

Finished Quilt Size

46" x 46"

Number of Blocks and Finished Size

5 sheep blocks	12" x 12"
4 Rail Fence blocks	12" x 12"

Fabric Requirements

Blue-green print	1½ yards*
Lavender print	½ yard
Purple print	1⅜ yards
White/purple print	¾ yard
White	¼ yard
Black	⅛ yard
Backing	2¾ yards

*Includes fabric for binding.

Number to Cut**

Template A	5 black
Template A rev.	5 black
Template B	10 black
Template C	5 black
Template D	5 white
Template E	5 lavender print
Template F	5 black
8½" squares (G)	5 blue-green print
2½" squares (H)	20 purple print
2½" x 8½" rectangle (I)	20 white/purple print
2½" x 6½" rectangle (J)	16 blue-green print
	16 lavender print
	16 white/purple print

**See Step 1 to cut borders before cutting other pieces.

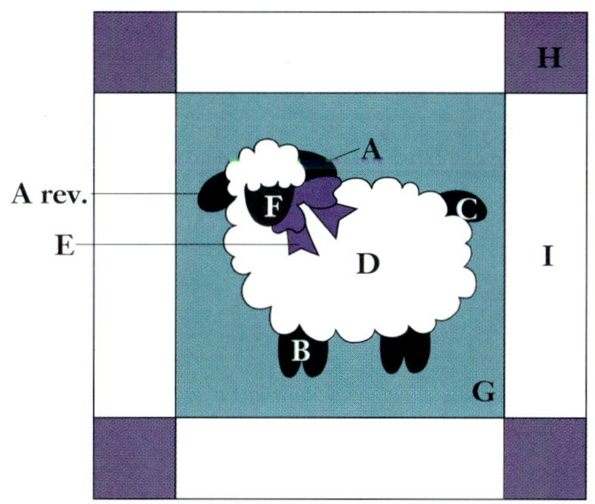

Appliqué Placement Diagram

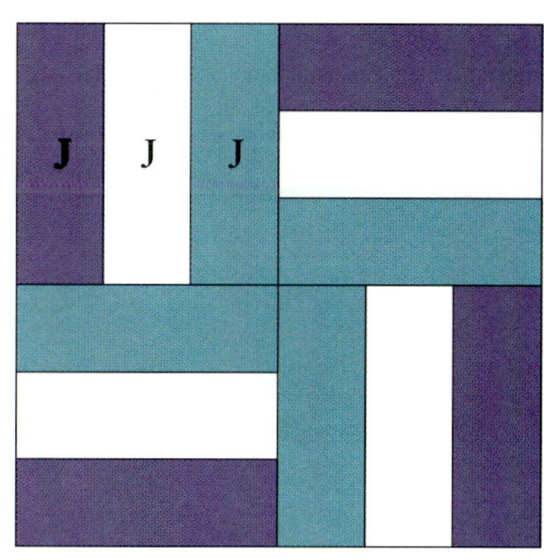

Block Assembly Diagram

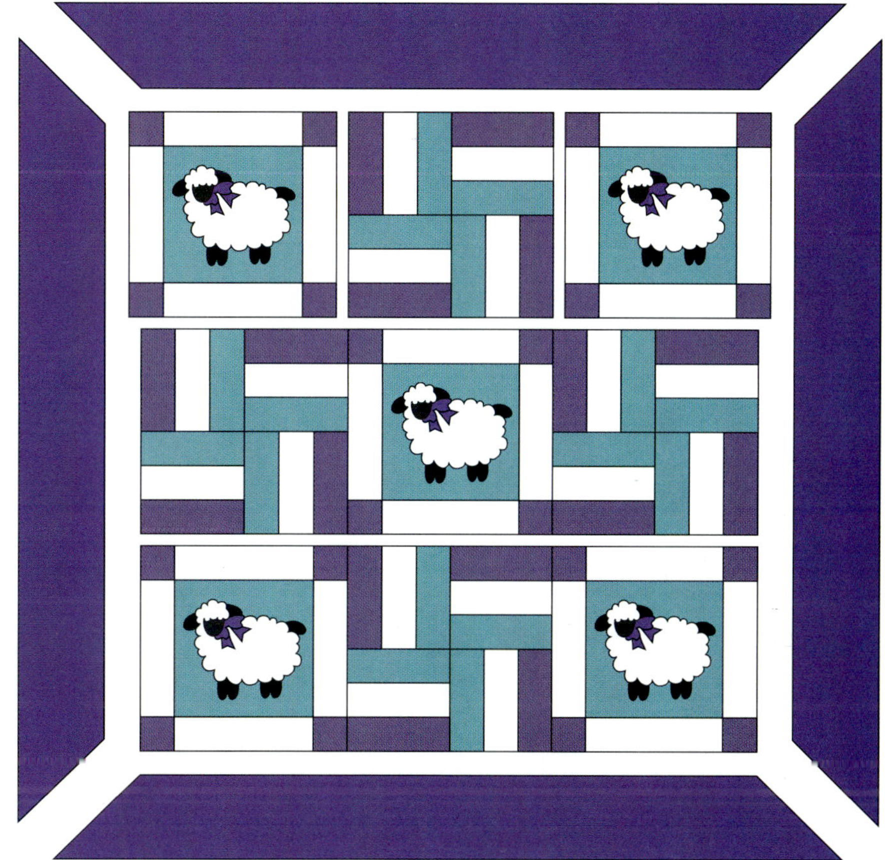

Setting Diagram

Quilt Top Assembly

1. From purple print, cut 4 (4½" x 44½") strips for border. Set aside.

2. To make 1 sheep block, arrange pieces A-F on G as shown in **Appliqué Placement Diagram.** Referring to instructions on pages 7-8, appliqué sheep pieces to G.

Join 1 I to top and 1 to bottom of G. To make side unit, join 1 H to each end of 1 I. Repeat to make 2 side units. Join 1 side unit to each side of I/G/I unit. Repeat to make 5 blocks.

3. Join 1 blue-green print J, 1 white/purple print J, and 1 lavender print J to make 1 Rail Fence unit. Repeat to make 4 units. Referring to **Block Assembly Diagram,** join units to form Rail Fence block. Repeat to make 4 blocks.

4. Referring to **Setting Diagram,** arrange blocks in 3 rows of 3 blocks, alternating sheep and Rail Fence blocks. Join blocks in rows. Join rows to assemble quilt top.

5. Mark centers on edges of each border strip. Mark centers on edges of quilt. Matching centers of borders and quilt edges, join 1 border strip to each edge. See page 8 for instructions on mitering border corners.

Quilting

Outline-quilt sheep. Add hearts and other quilting as desired.

Finished Edges

Referring to instructions on page 11, make 5¼ yards of 2½"-wide bias binding from blue-green print. Apply binding to quilt edges.

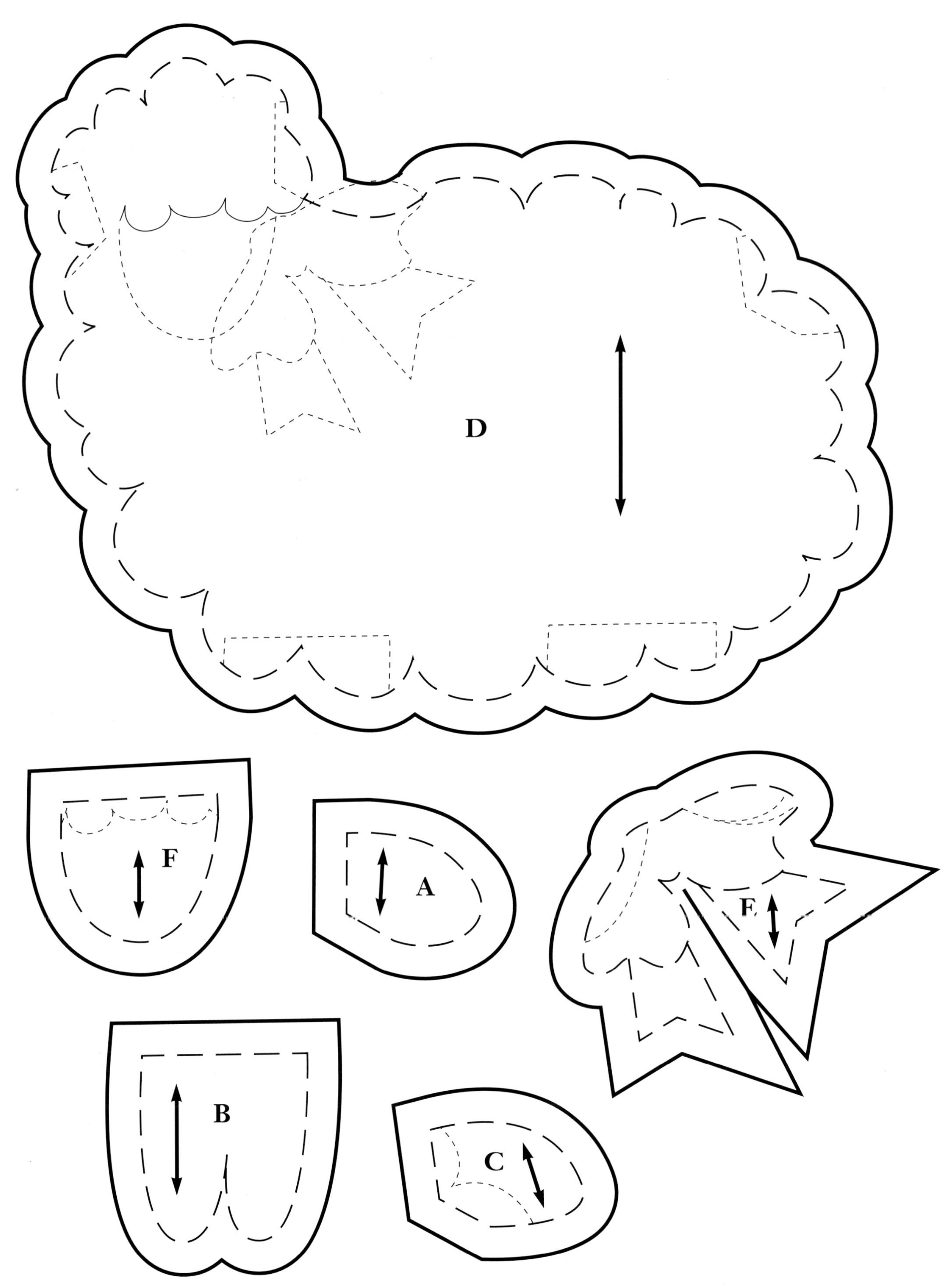
D
F
A
E
B
C

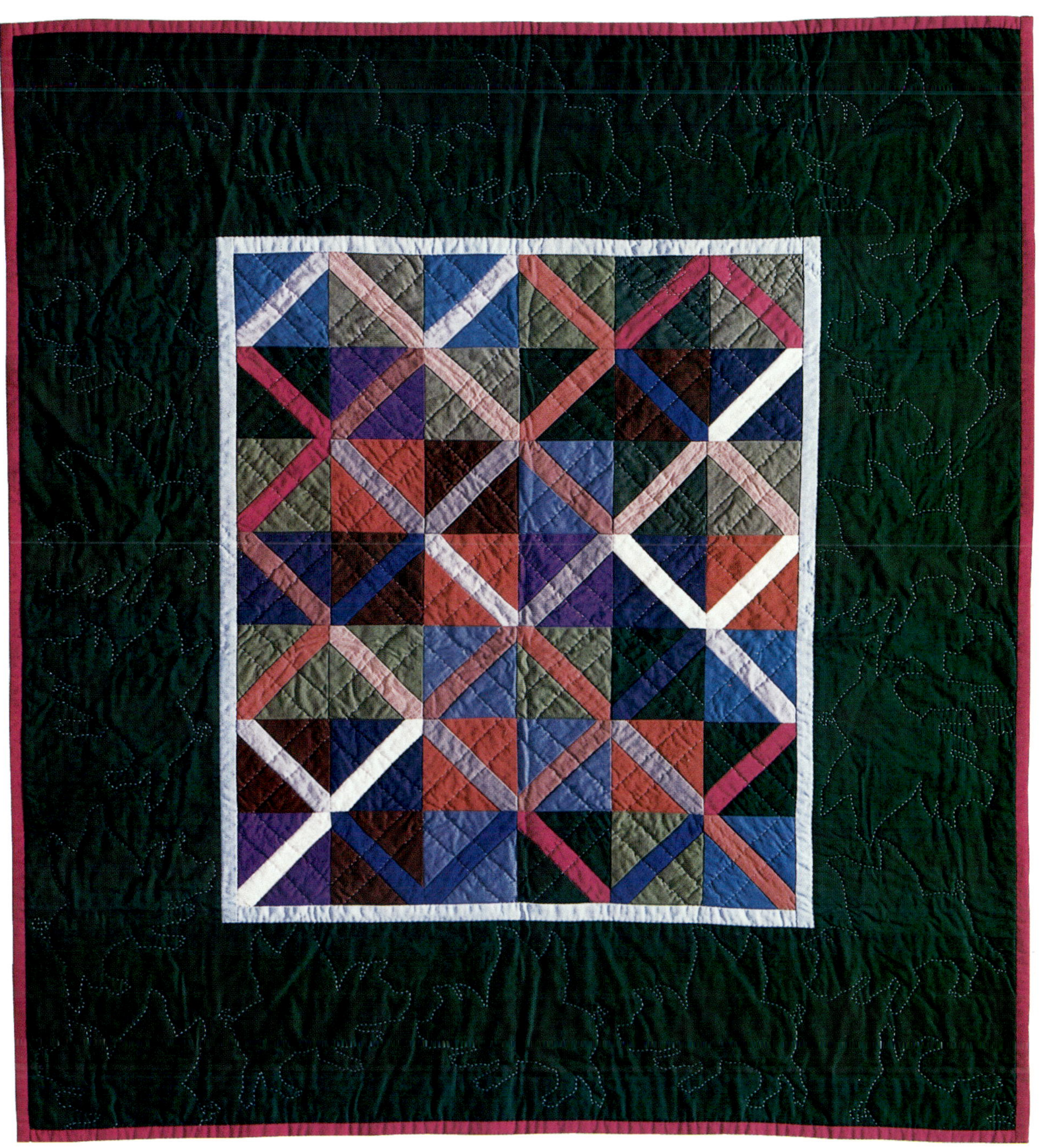

Quilt by Marta Amundson
Riverton, Wyoming

When Pigs Have Wings

Marta Amundson combines her sense of humor and her love of animals in this quilt. The wide borders provide ample space for her quilted silhouettes. "I designed this quilt to represent those times when I just can't compromise anymore," she says, "and I make the decision to stand my ground until *pigs have wings!*"

Finished Quilt Size

41½" x 45½"

Number of Blocks and Finished Size

42 blocks 4" x 4"

Fabric Requirements

Assorted solids	1¼ yards total
Lavender	¼ yard
Dark green	1½ yards
Fuchsia for binding	¾ yard
Backing	1½ yards

Number to Cut*

Template A	84 assorted solids

*To rotary-cut, cut 21 (6¼") squares. Then cut squares diagonally into quarters to form 84 quarter-square triangles.

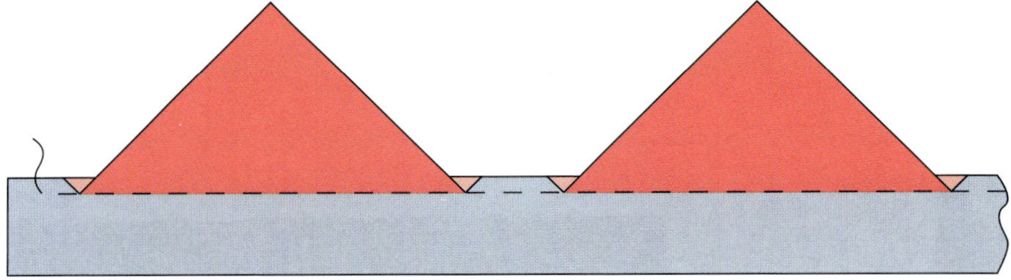

Figure 1

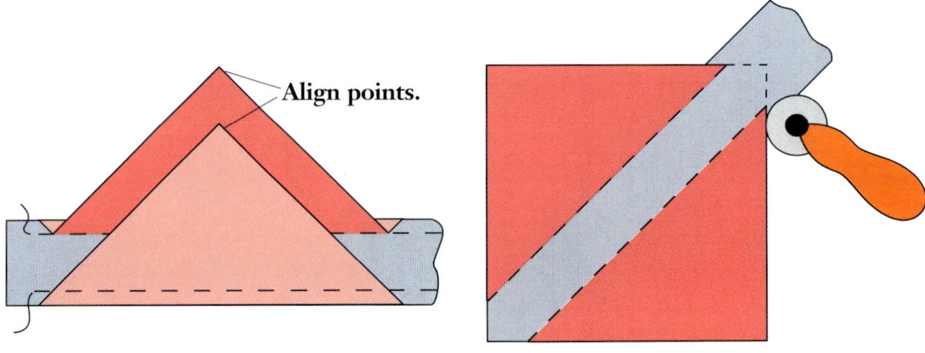

Figure 2

Figure 3

Block Assembly Diagram

Quilt Top Assembly

1. Cut a total of 9 yards of 1½"-wide strips from assorted solids. Referring to **Block Assembly Diagram, Figure 1,** join 42 As to 1½"-wide strips, leaving approximately ½" between triangles and varying color combinations. Referring to **Figure 2,** join remaining As to opposite side of 1½"-wide strips, aligning top points of triangles and matching colors. Referring to **Figure 3,** trim corners to square off blocks.

3. Referring to photograph, arrange blocks in 7 horizontal rows of 6 blocks so that diagonal bars form Xs. When satisfied with color placement, join blocks in rows. Join rows to assemble quilt top.

4. From lavender, cut 4 (1¼" wide) crosswise strips for inner border. From dark green, cut 4 (8½"-wide) crosswise strips for outer border. Join inner border strips to top and bottom edges of quilt. Then join remaining inner border strips to sides of quilt. Join outer border strips to sides of quilt. Join remaining outer border strips to top and bottom edges of quilt.

Quilting

Quilt in-the-ditch along outside seams of diagonal bars and inner border. Referring to photograph, quilt lattice pattern over blocks. Quilt pig with wings pattern in outer borders as desired.

Finished Edges

Referring to instructions on page 11, make 5 yards of 2½"-wide bias or straight-grain binding from fuchsia. Apply binding to quilt edges.

A

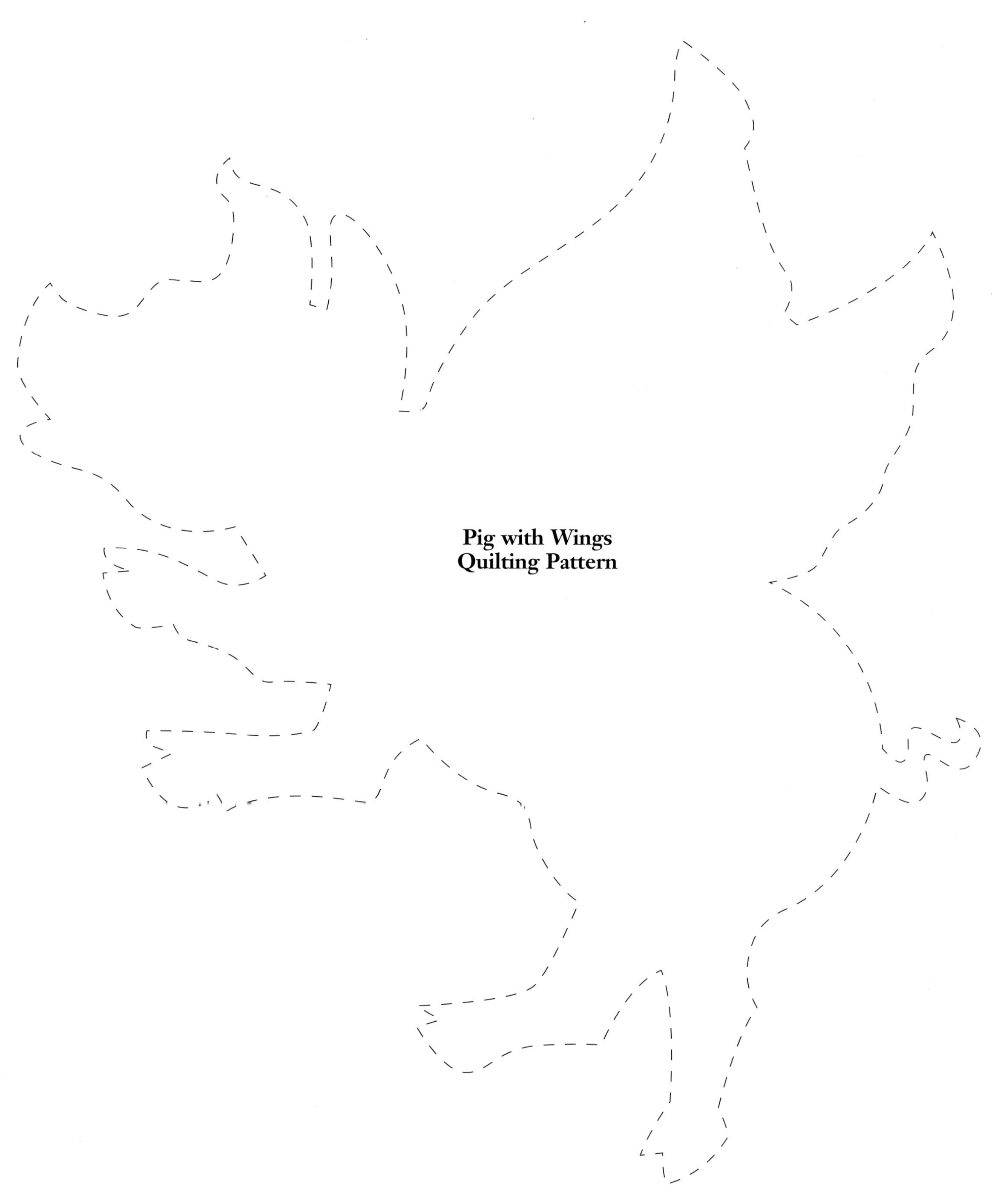
Pig with Wings
Quilting Pattern

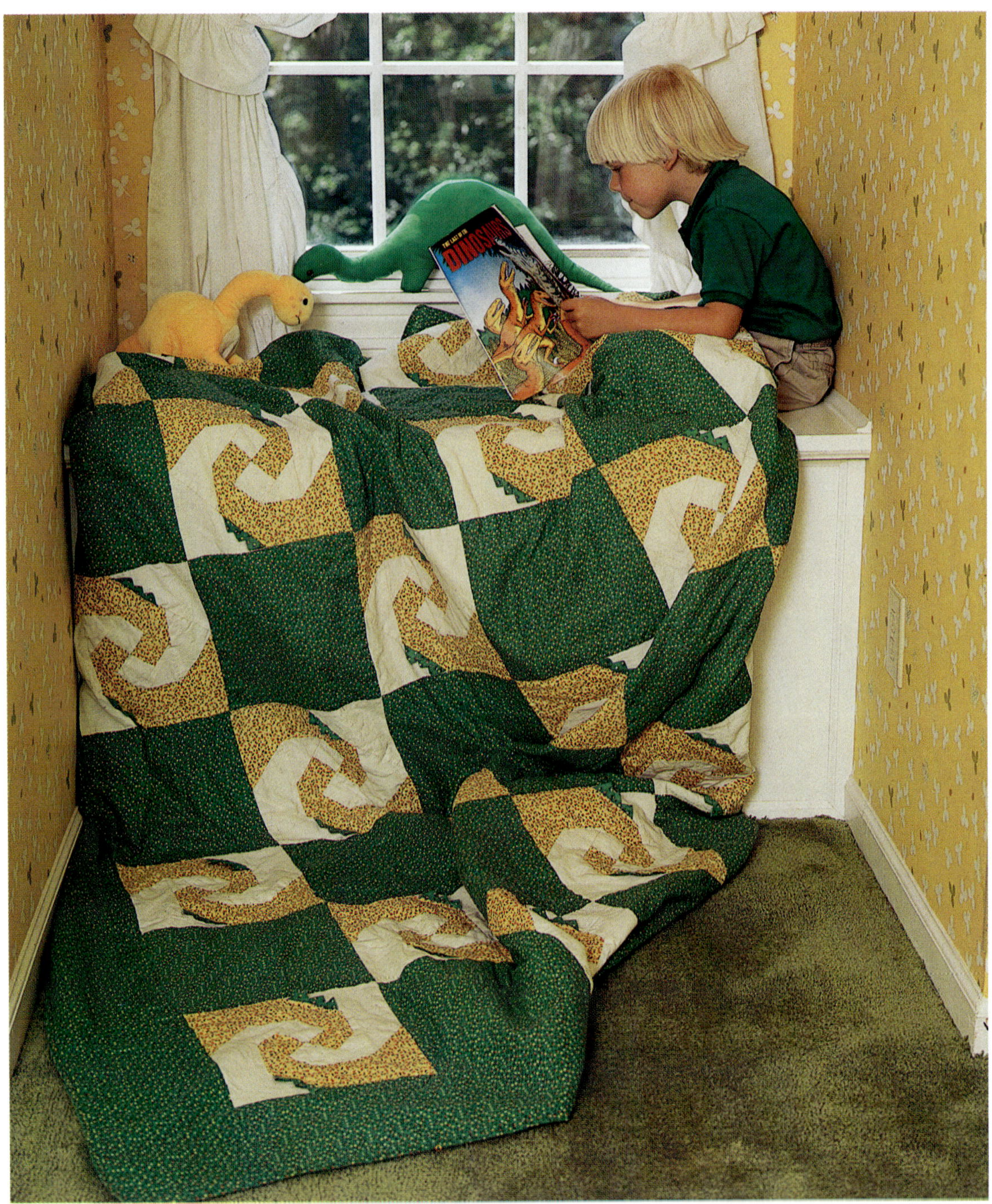

Quilt by Norma E. Davis
Colorado Springs, Colorado

Kissing Dinosaurs

Kissing Dinosaurs was Norma Davis's first quilt. When Norma saw an example of a Monkey Wrench block, she saw dinosaurs instead of monkeys. "My grandson, Aaron, is crazy about dinosaurs," says Norma. "So I added prairie points for the dinosaur's spikes, and there was my dinosaur." Norma suggests using a lightweight cotton for the prairie points to make folding easier.

Finished Quilt Size

72" x 92"

Number of Blocks and Finished Size

24 dinosaur blocks 10" x 10"

Fabric Requirements

Yellow print	1½ yards
Green print	5 yards*
Lightweight green print for spikes	½ yard
Muslin	1½ yards
Backing	5½ yards

*Includes fabric for binding.

Number to Cut**

Template A†	48 yellow print 48 muslin
Template B†	48 yellow print 48 muslin
Template C†	48 yellow print 48 muslin
Template D†	48 yellow print 48 muslin

**See Step 1 to cut borders before cutting other pieces.

† See Alternate Rotary-Cutting Instructions on page 20 before cutting.

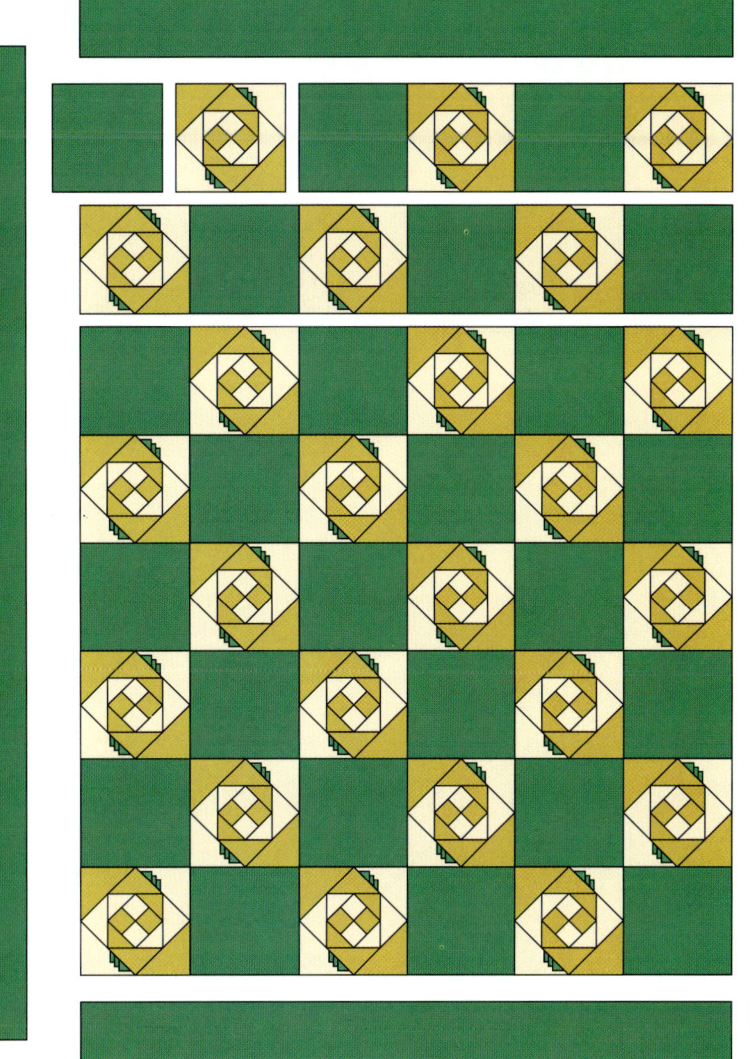

Setting Diagram

Quilt Top Assembly

1. From green print, cut 2 (6½" x 60½") strips and 2 (6½" x 92½") strips for border. Set aside.

2. Cut 3 (2") squares from lightweight green print. Fold each square in half diagonally to form triangle. Fold triangle in half to make dinosaur spike. Referring to **Spike Placement Diagram,** overlap 3 spikes along right side of 1 yellow print C. Stitch spikes in place. Repeat to make spikes on remaining yellow print Cs. Set aside.

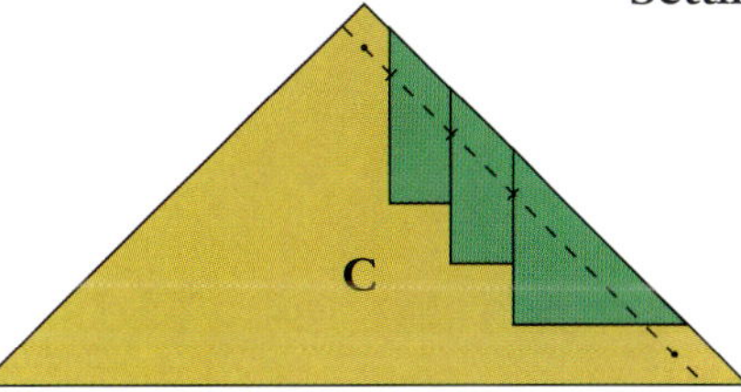

Spike Placement Diagram

3. Referring to **Block Assembly Diagram,** join 2 yellow print As to 2 muslin As to make a square. Join 2 yellow print Bs and 2 muslin Bs to sides of square. Join 2 yellow print and 2 muslin Cs to unit, making sure spike placement is correct. Join 2 yellow print Ds and 2 muslin Ds to unit to complete block. Repeat to make 24 dinosaur blocks.

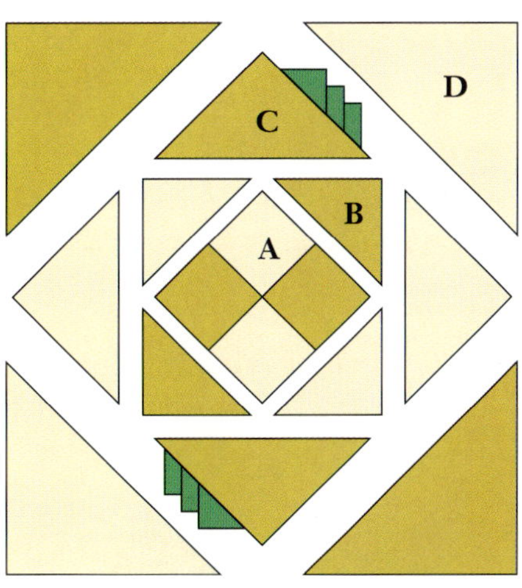

Block Assembly Diagram

4. Cut 24 (10½") squares from green print. Referring to **Setting Diagram,** alternate 3 green print squares with 3 dinosaur blocks. Join blocks to make 8 horizontal rows of 6 blocks. Join rows to assemble quilt top.

5. Join (6½" x 60") borders to top and bottom edges of quilt. Join (6½" x 92½") borders to sides of quilt.

Quilting

Outline-quilt ¼" inside dinosaur seam lines. Quilt parallel diagonal lines in green print squares.

Finished Edges

Referring to instructions on page 11, make 9¼ yards of 2½"-wide bias or straight-grain binding from green print. Apply binding to quilt edges.

Alternate Rotary-Cutting Instructions

1. For A, cut 2 ($2\frac{1}{4}$" x 45") strips and 1 ($2\frac{1}{4}$" x 8") strip from yellow print. Cut strips into 48 ($2\frac{1}{4}$") squares. Repeat to make 48 ($2\frac{1}{4}$") muslin squares.

2. For B, cut 2 ($3\frac{3}{8}$" x 45") strips from yellow print. Cut strips into 24 ($3\frac{3}{8}$") squares. Cut squares diagonally in half to form 48 triangles. Repeat to make 48 muslin triangles.

3. For C, cut 2 ($4\frac{3}{8}$" x 45") strips and 1 ($4\frac{3}{8}$" x $17\frac{1}{2}$") strip from yellow print. Cut strips into 24 ($4\frac{3}{8}$") squares. Cut squares diagonally in half to form 48 triangles. Repeat to make 48 muslin triangles.

4. For D, cut 3 ($5\frac{7}{8}$" x 45") strips and 1 ($5\frac{7}{8}$" x 18") strip from yellow print. Cut strips into 24 ($5\frac{7}{8}$") squares. Cut squares diagonally in half to form 48 triangles. Repeat to make 48 muslin triangles.

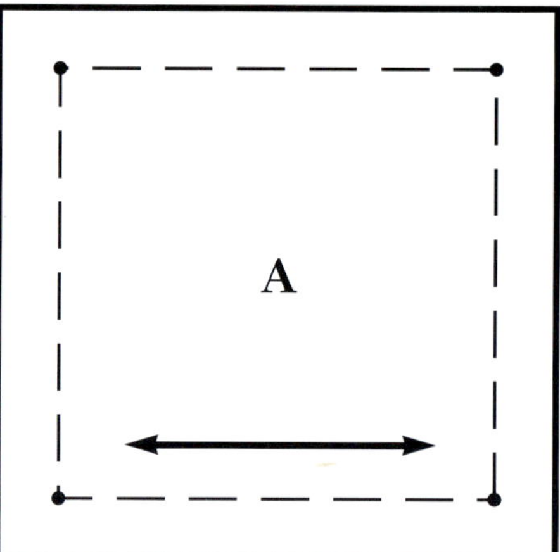

B

C

D

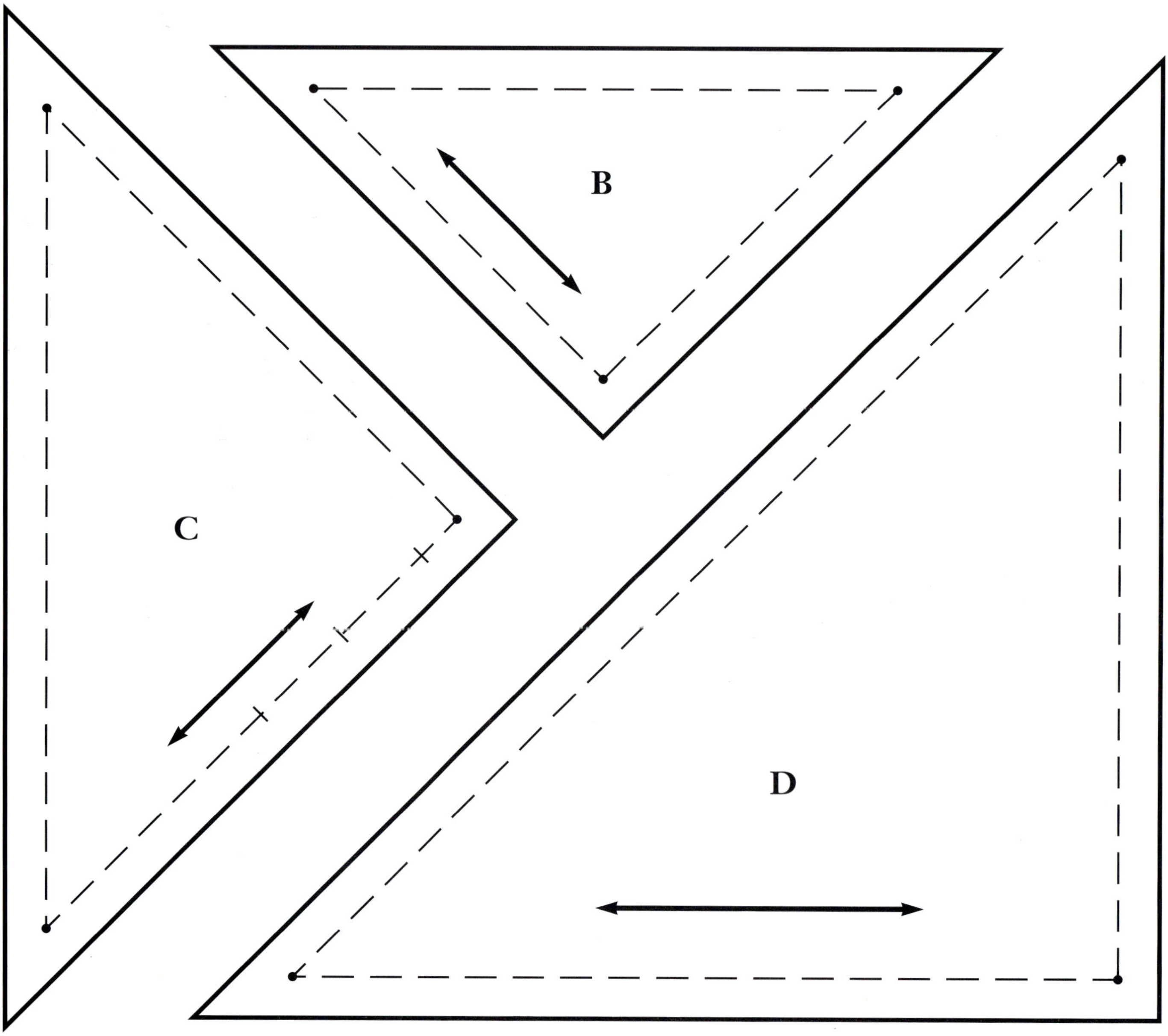

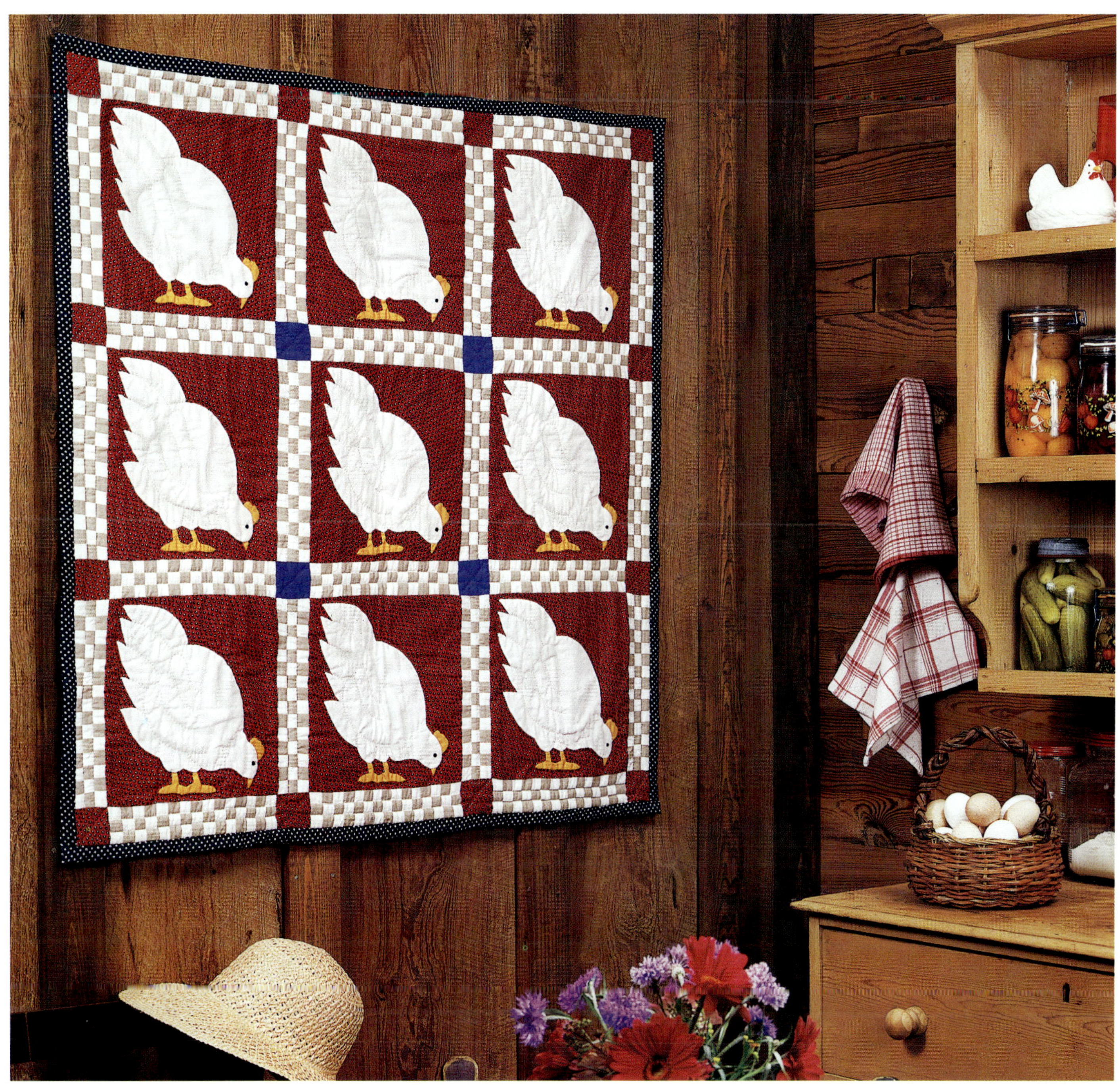

Quilt by Jane Eakin
Wilmette, Illinois

Hens A-Peckin'

Anyone who has fed chickens or gathered eggs can relate to Jane Eakin's lighthearted quilt. She used strip piecing to create the checkerboard sashing, which is reminiscent of old feed sacks. With the help of Phyllis Sylvester, Emma Yoder, and Vivian Walsh, Jane's wall hanging was as easy to make as scrambled eggs!

Finished Quilt Size

44" x 44"

Number of Blocks and Finished Size

9 chicken blocks 11¼" x 11¼"

Fabric Requirements

Red print	1¼ yards
White	2¼ yards
Gold	⅛ yard
Tan	1¼ yards
Blue	⅛ yard
Navy print for binding	¾ yard
Backing	2¾ yards

Other Materials

Red quilting thread
Black embroidery floss

Number to Cut

Template A	9 white
Template B	9 gold
Template C	9 gold
Template D	9 gold
Template E	4 blue
	12 red print

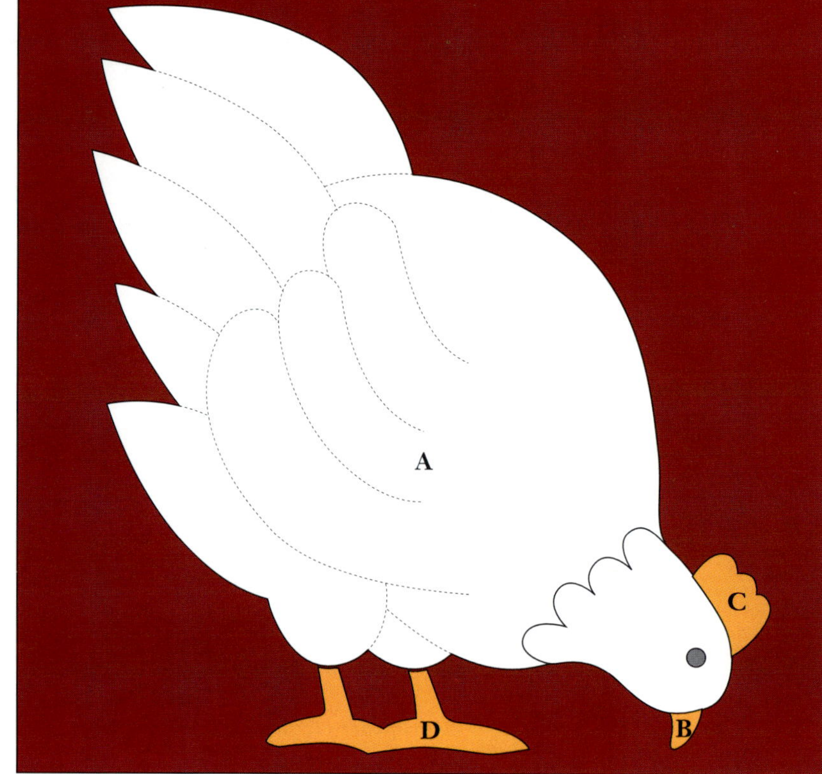

Appliqué Placement Diagram

Quilt Top Assembly

1. Using 3 strands of embroidery floss, satin-stitch 1 eye on each chicken (A).

Cut 9 (11¾") squares from red print. Referring to **Appliqué Placement Diagram,** center 1 A on each red square and appliqué, leaving beak, comb, and feet areas unsewn. Appliqué beak (B), comb (C), and feet (D). Finish appliquéing A by stitching down areas left unsewn. Repeat to make 9 squares.

2. Cut 33 (44" x 1¼") strips each from white and tan. Referring to **Checkerboard Sashing Strip Diagram, Figure 1,** join 1 white strip, 1 tan strip, and 1 white strip along long edges. Referring to **Figure 2,** repeat process with 1 tan strip, 1 white strip, and 1 tan strip. Cut across strips to make 35 (1¼"-wide) units. Beginning and ending with white/tan/white units, join 15 units together, alternating colors to form checkerboard sashing strip **(Figure 3)**. Repeat to make 24 checkerboard sashing strips.

3. Beginning and ending with checkerboard sashing strips, alternate 4 sashing strips with 3 chicken squares to form 1 row. Repeat to make 3 rows.

4. To make top sashing row, alternate 4 red sashing squares with 3 checkerboard sashing strips, beginning and ending with squares. Repeat to make bottom sashing row.

To make inner sashing row, join 1 red square, 1 strip, 1 blue square,

Figure 1

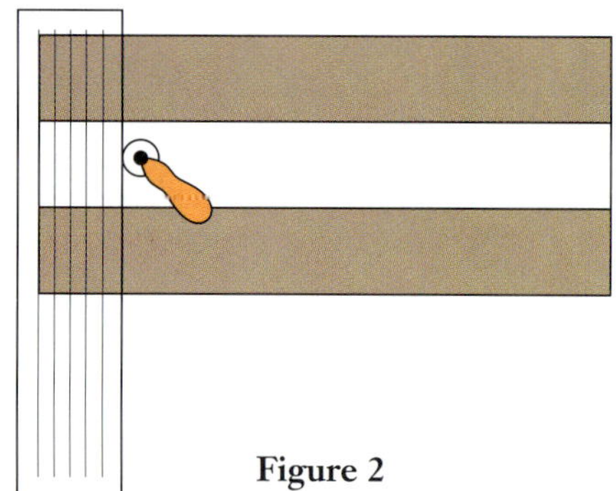

Figure 2

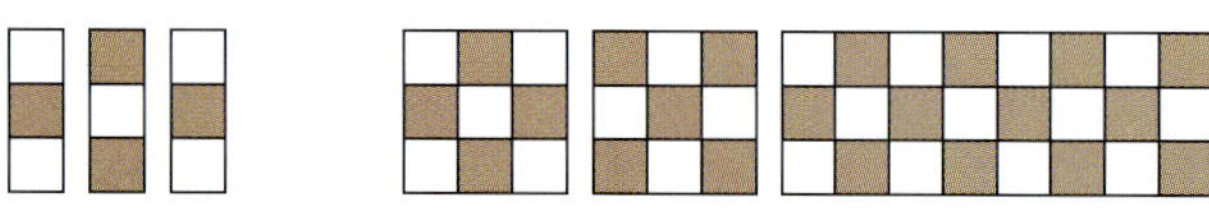

Figure 3

Checkerboard Sashing Strip Diagram

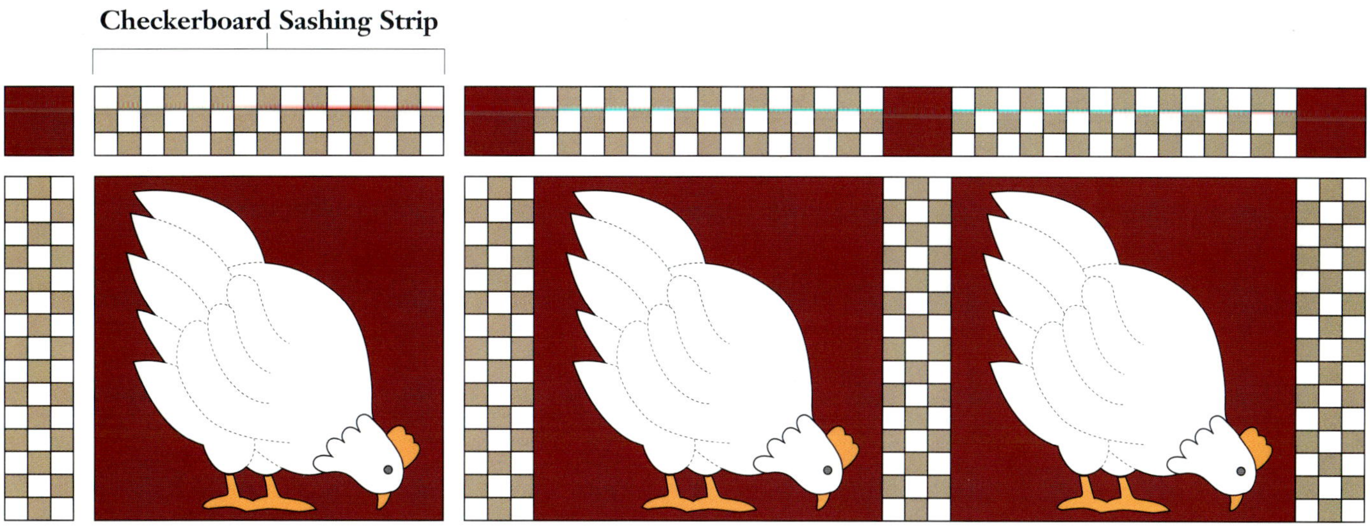

Checkerboard Sashing Strip

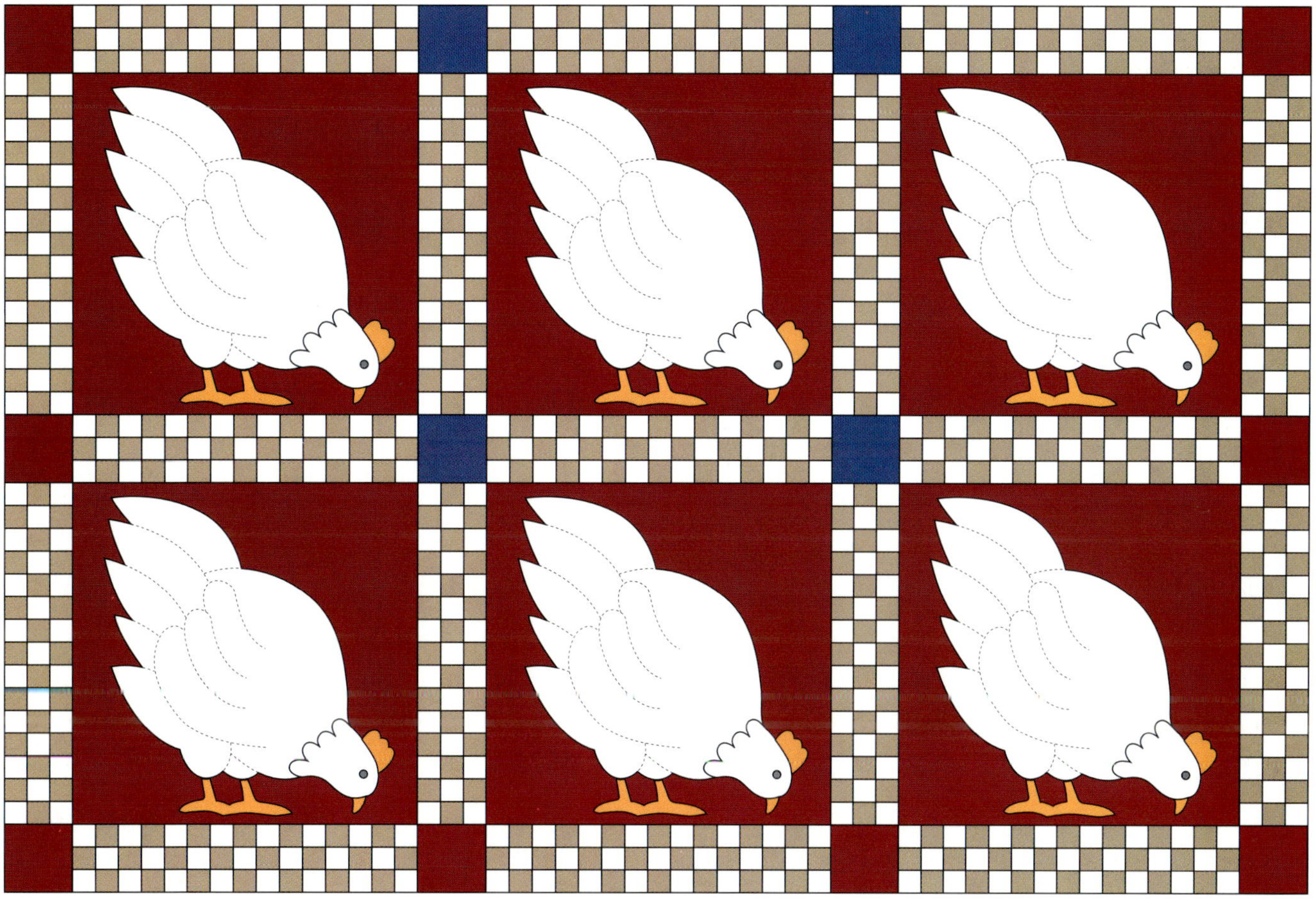

Setting Diagram

1 strip, 1 blue square, 1 strip, and 1 red square. Repeat to make 2 inner sashing rows.

5. Referring to **Setting Diagram,** alternate sashing rows and chicken rows. Join rows to assemble quilt top.

Quilting

Quilt feathers on each chicken. Outline-quilt chickens and seams of blocks. Quilt Xs in sashing squares.

Finished Edges

Referring to instructions on page 11, make 5 yards of 2½"-wide bias or straight-grain binding from navy print. Apply binding to quilt edges.

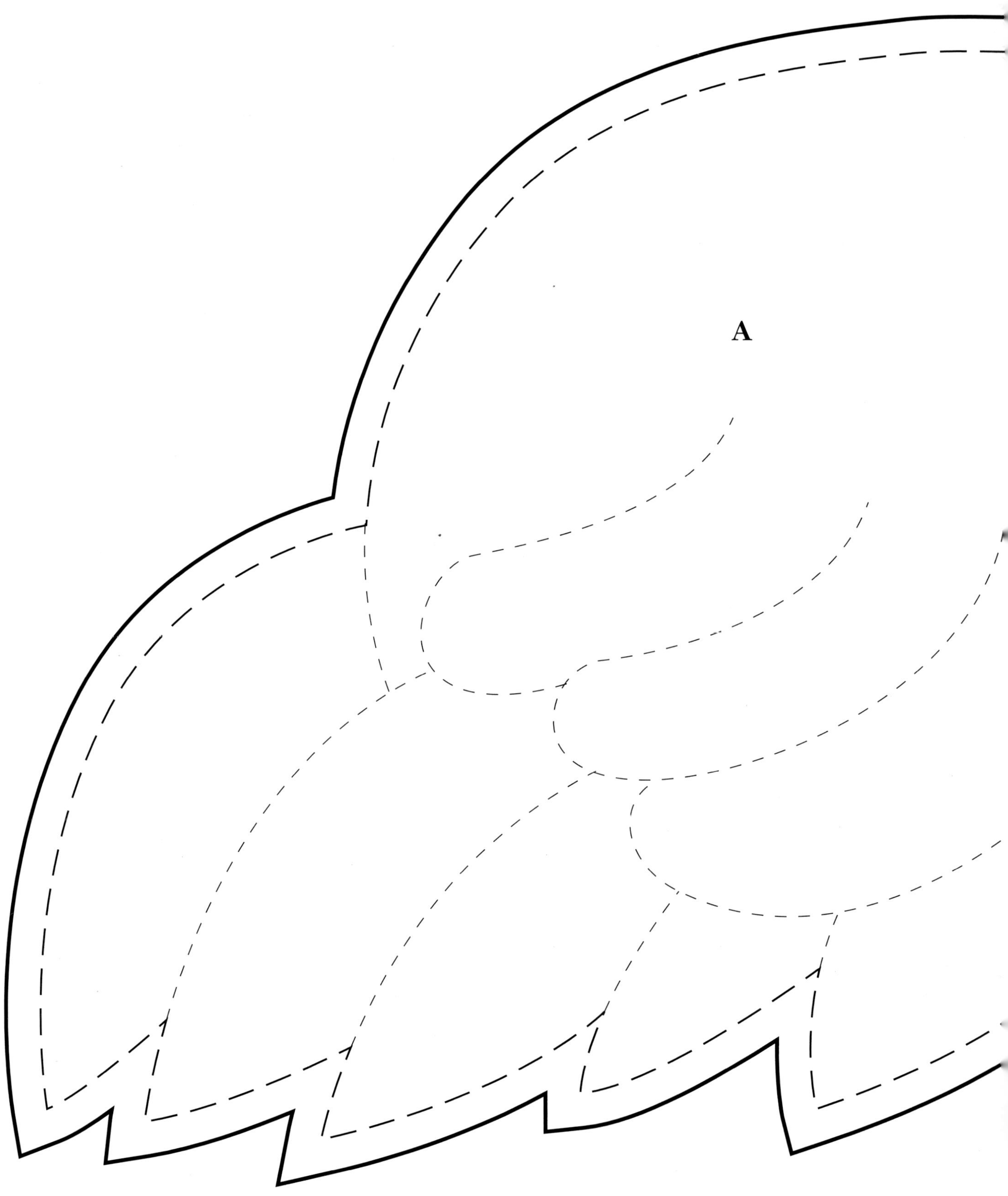
A

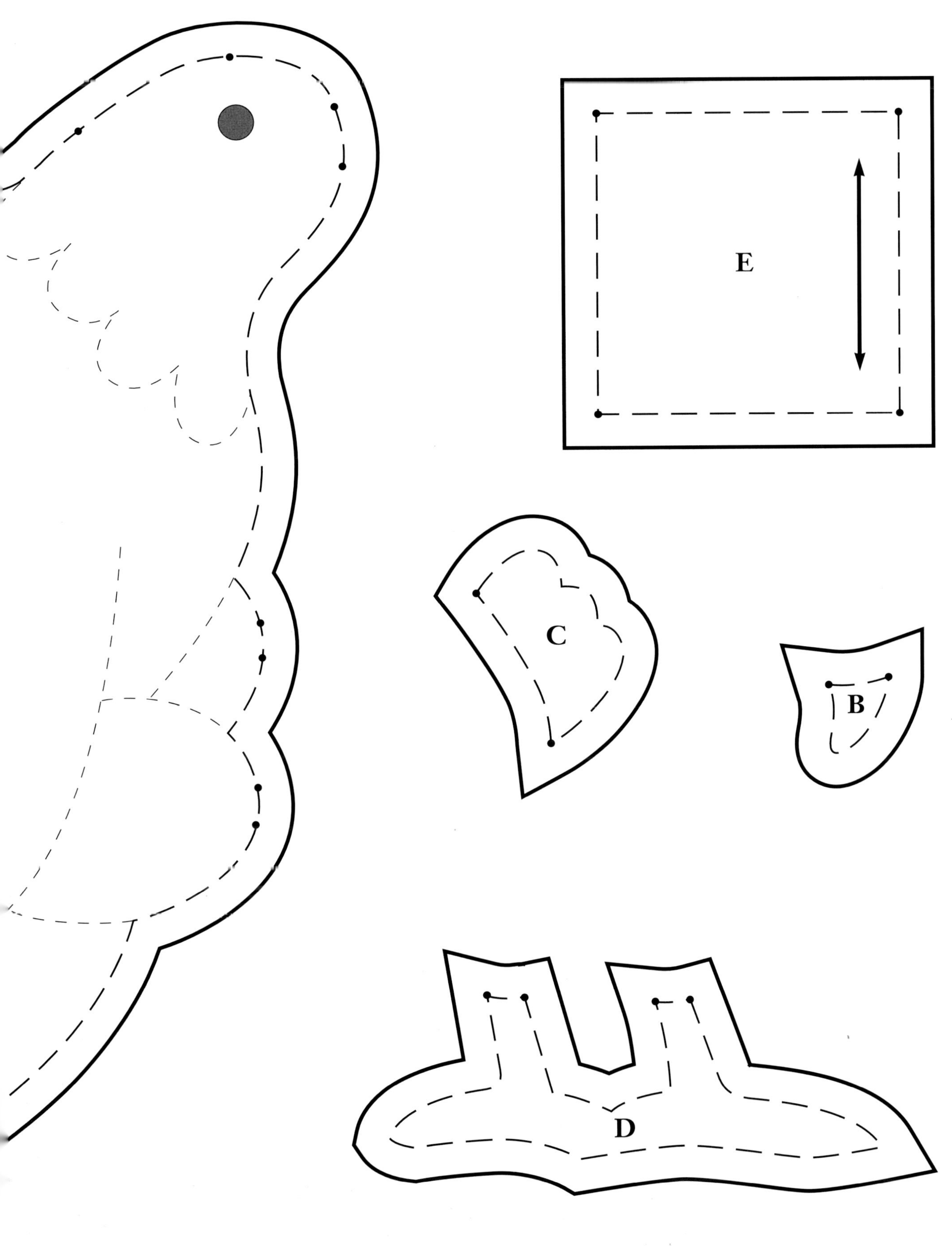
E
C
B
D

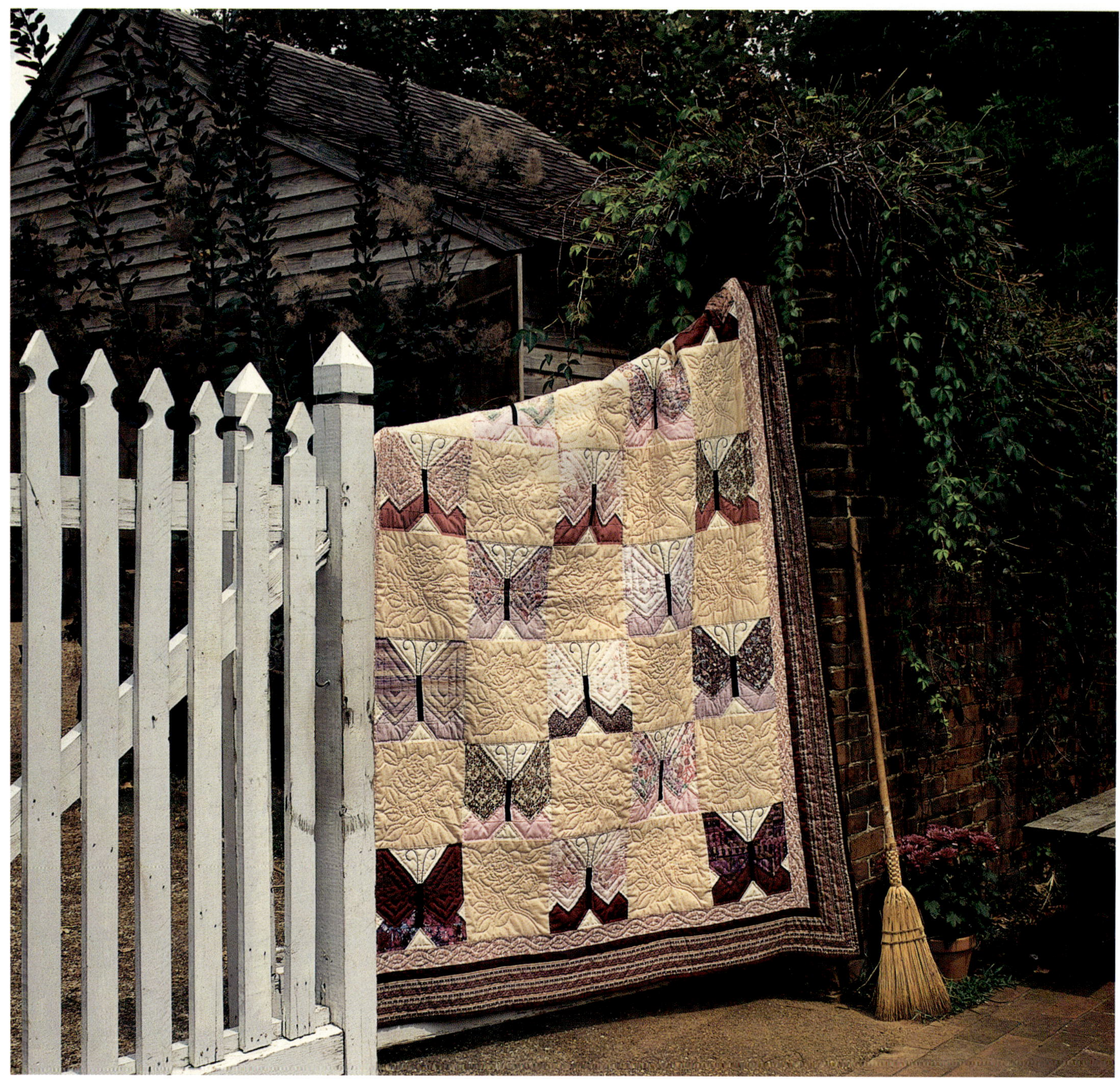

Quilt by June Wolpert
Nashville, Indiana

McKim Butterflies

June Wolpert calls her quilt *McKim Butterflies* in honor of Ruby S. McKim, owner of McKim Studios of Independence, Missouri. McKim Studios syndicated a newspaper column of quilt patterns during the twenties and thirties. June discovered this pattern when Dover Publications reprinted a pamphlet containing McKim patterns, *101 Patchwork Patterns*, in 1962.

Finished Quilt Size

64" x 84"

Number of Blocks and Finished Size

18 butterfly blocks 10" x 10"

Fabric Requirements

Beige	1¾ yards
Muslin	¾ yard
Assorted medium prints	1⅜ yards total
Assorted darks	1 yard total
Black	⅛ yard
Burgundy/white print	2¼ yards
Burgundy	3¼ yards*
Burgundy stripe	2½ yards
Backing	5 yards

*Includes fabric for binding.

Other Materials

Black embroidery floss

Number to Cut**

Template A	18 muslin
Template B	18 medium prints
Template B rev.	18 medium prints
Template C	36 medium prints
Template D	36 muslin
Template E	36 assorted darks
Template F	18 assorted darks
Template F rev.	18 assorted darks
Template G	18 black
Template H	18 assorted darks
Template H rev.	18 assorted darks
Template I	18 muslin

**Select 1 medium print and 1 dark for each butterfly.

Quilt Top Assembly

1. Referring to **Block Assembly Diagram,** join 1 B and 1 B rev. to 1 A to form top block unit.

A
B
B rev.
G
C
C
D
E
F
F rev.
D
H
I
H rev.

Block Assembly Diagram

2. Referring to **Block Assembly Diagram,** join 1 D to 1 E. Repeat to make 2 D/E units. Join 1 D/E unit and 1 F to 1 C. Join remaining D/E unit and 1 F rev. to 1 C. Join D/E/C/F unit and D/E/C/F rev. unit to 1 G to make middle block unit.

3. Referring to **Block Assembly Diagram,** join 1 H and 1 H rev. to 1 I to form bottom block unit. Join top, middle, and bottom block units to complete block. Using 3 strands of black floss, backstitch antennae.

4. Repeat steps 1–4 to make 18 butterfly blocks.

5. From beige, cut 17 (10½") squares. Referring to **Setting Diagram,** alternate butterfly blocks with beige squares. Join blocks to make 7 horizontal rows of 5 blocks. Join rows to assemble quilt top.

6. From burgundy/white print, cut 2 (2½" x 56") and 2 (2½" x 76") strips for inner borders. Mark centers on edges of each border strip. Mark centers on edges of quilt. Matching centers of borders and quilt edges, join border strips to all edges. See page 8 for instructions on mitering border corners.

7. From burgundy, cut 2 (1½" x 58") and 2 (1½" x 78") strips for middle borders. Mark centers and join to quilt as described in Step 6.

8. From burgundy stripe, cut 2 (4½" x 66") and 2 (4½" x 86") strips for outer borders. Mark centers and join to quilt as described in Step 6.

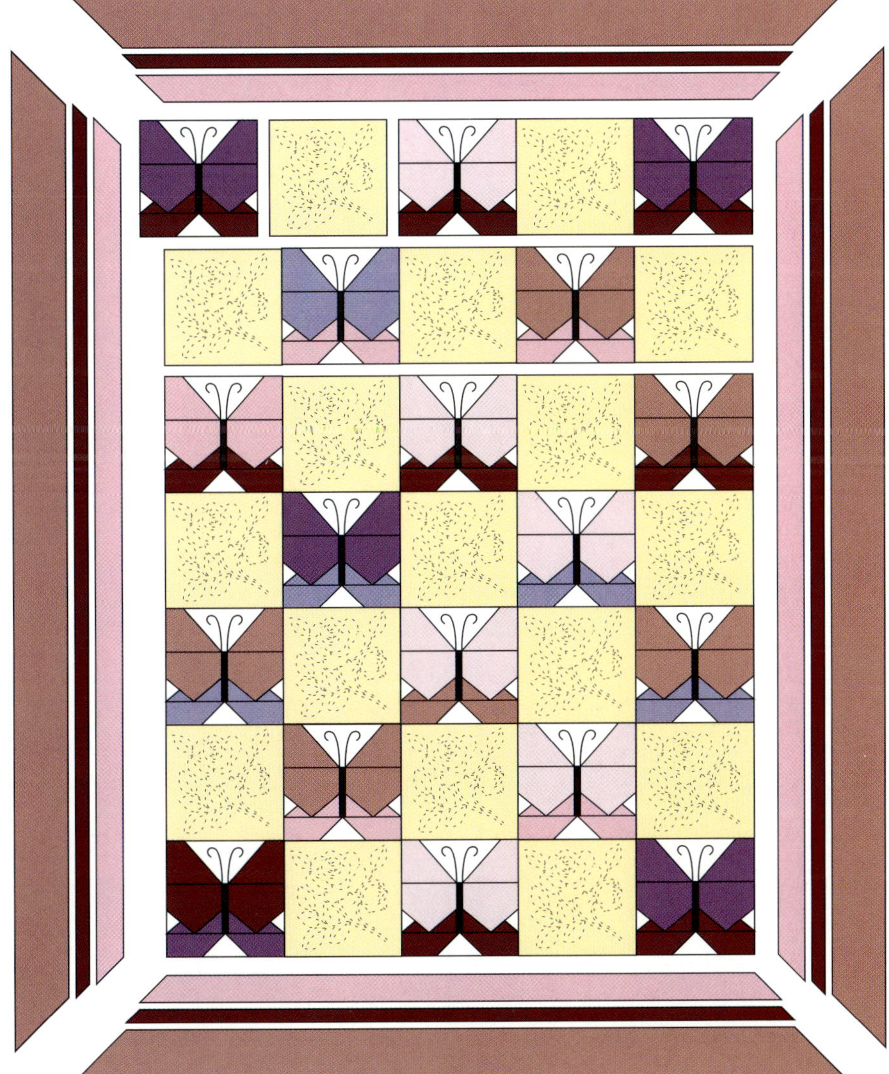

Setting Diagram

Quilting

Outline-quilt butterflies. Quilt rose pattern in beige squares.

Finished Edges

Referring to instructions on page 11, make 8½ yards of 2½"-wide bias or straight-grain binding from burgundy. Apply binding to quilt edges.

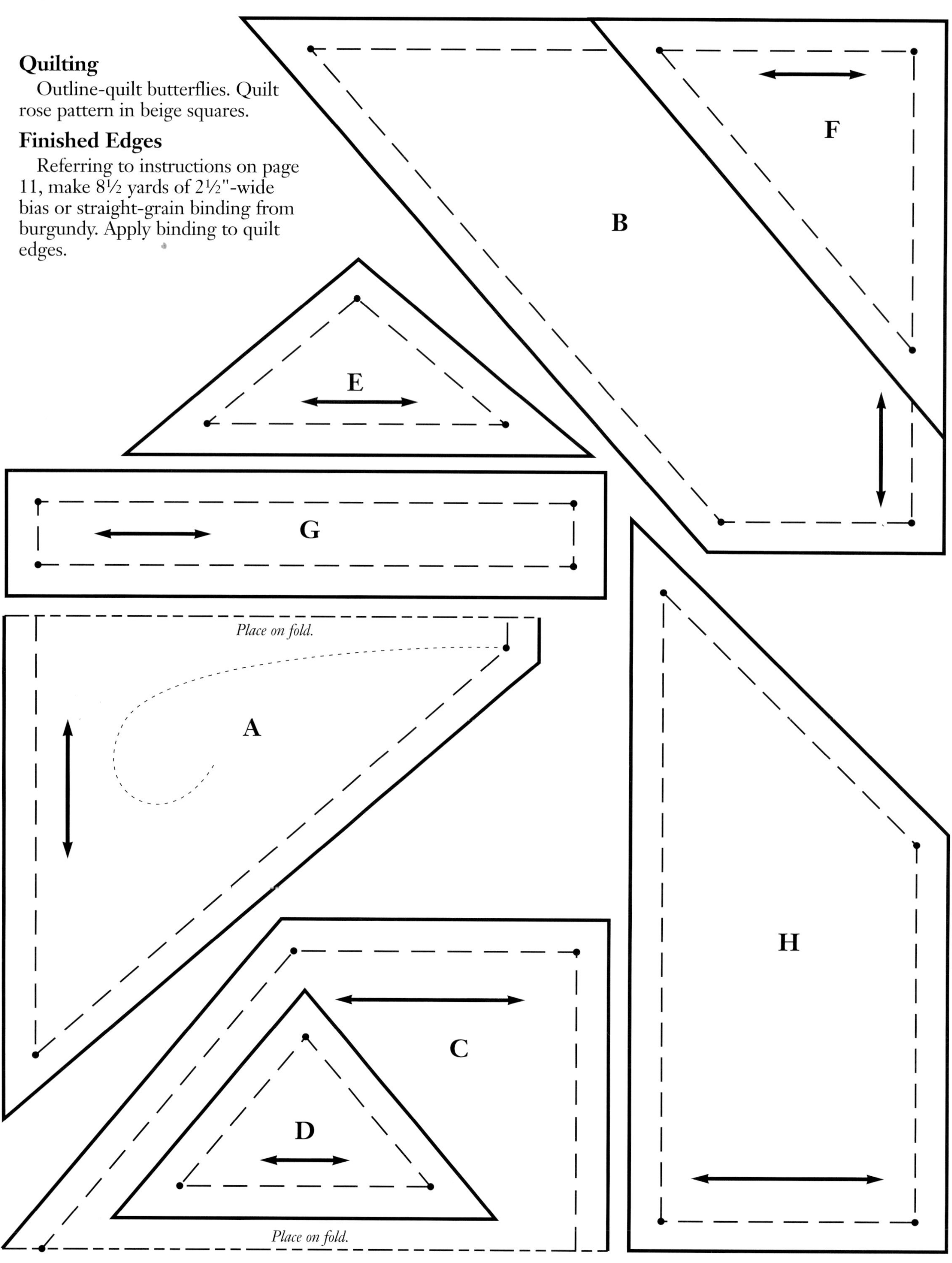

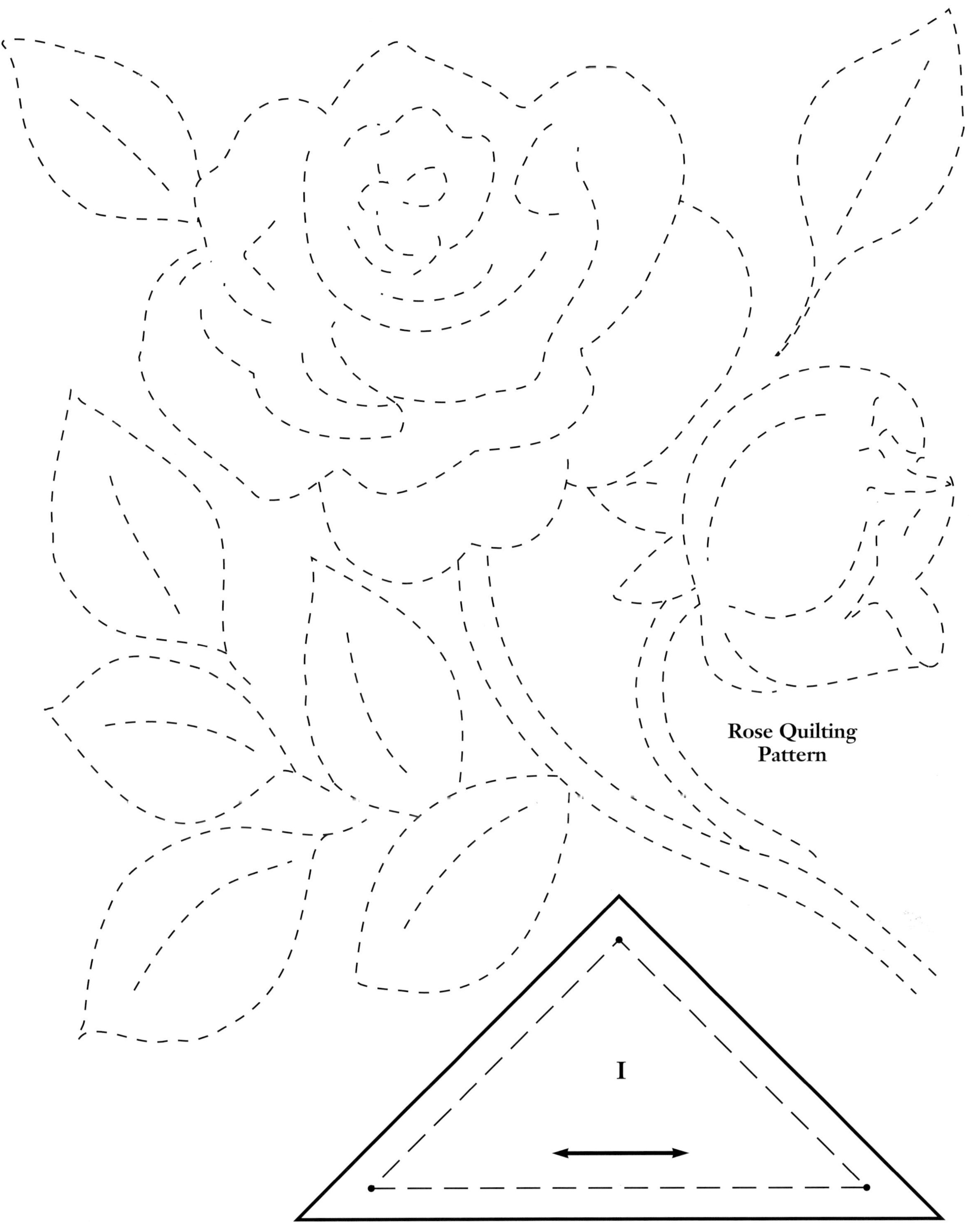
Rose Quilting Pattern
I

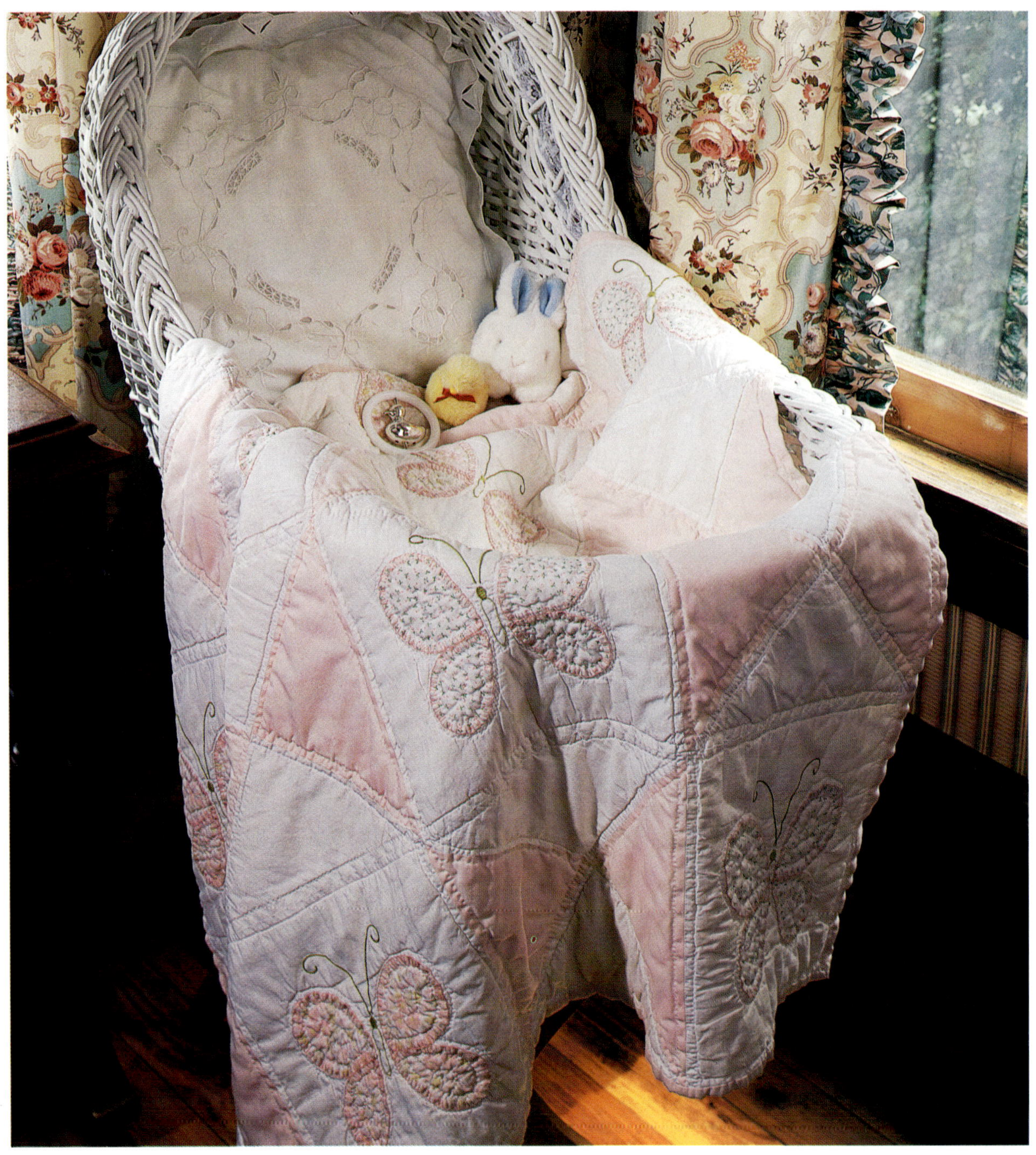

Quilt by Patricia Ramey Channell
Leeds, Alabama

Buttonhole Butterflies

This butterfly crib quilt makes a perfect cocoon for a new arrival. Geometric blocks echo the appliquéd shapes of floating butterflies. Ramey Channell used buttonhole appliqué to add interest to her original design.

Finished Size

37" x 46¼"

Number of Blocks and Finished Size

10 butterfly blocks	9¼" x 9¼"
10 hourglass blocks	9¼" x 9¼"

Fabric Requirements

White	1¾ yards
Pink	1 yard*
Assorted pink prints	½ yard total
Backing	1½ yards

*Includes fabric for binding.

Other Materials

Green embroidery floss
Pink embroidery floss

Number to Cut

Template A	10 assorted pink prints
Template A rev.	10 assorted pink prints
Template B	10 assorted pink prints
Template B rev.	10 assorted pink prints
10½" square	5 pink 5 white
9¾" square	10 white

Quilt Top Assembly

1. Cut each 10½" square in quarters diagonally to get 20 pink and 20 white triangles. Referring to photograph, join 1 pink triangle to 1 white triangle. Repeat to make 20 pieced triangles. Join 2 pieced triangles, alternating colors, to make a square. Repeat to make 10 squares. Set aside.

2. Fold 1 (9¾") square in half vertically and horizontally, finger-pressing folds to establish placement guidelines. Position square over **Appliqué Placement Diagram,** matching center of square with marked center on pattern. Lightly trace embroidery details and wing outlines. Using 2 strands of green floss, outline-stitch butterfly body and antennae. Satin-stitch head.

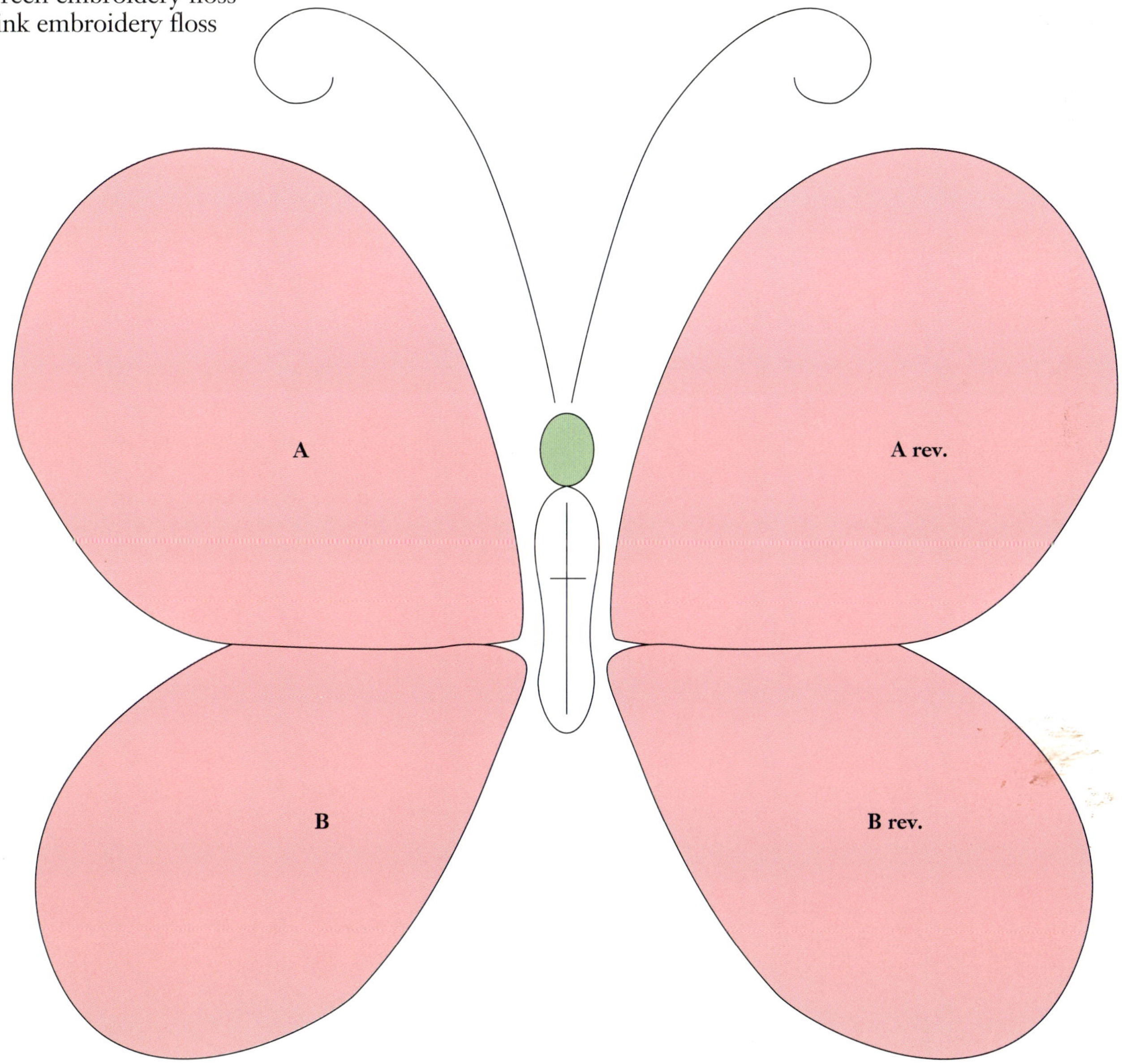

A

A rev.

B

B rev.

Appliqué Placement Diagram

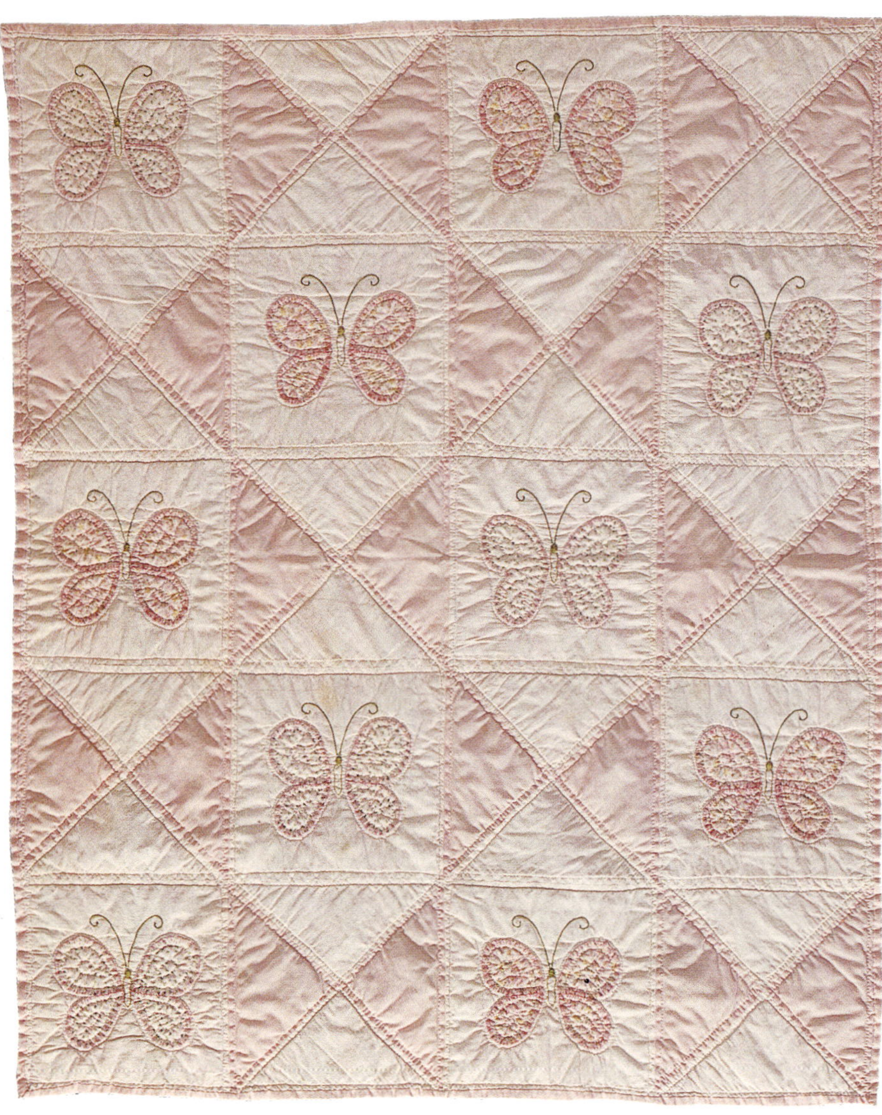

3. Position A and A rev. on square, aligning edges with traced outlines. Referring to **Buttonhole Stitch Diagram** and using 2 strands of pink floss, work small buttonhole stitches around edges of A and A rev. Appliqué B and B rev. in same manner.

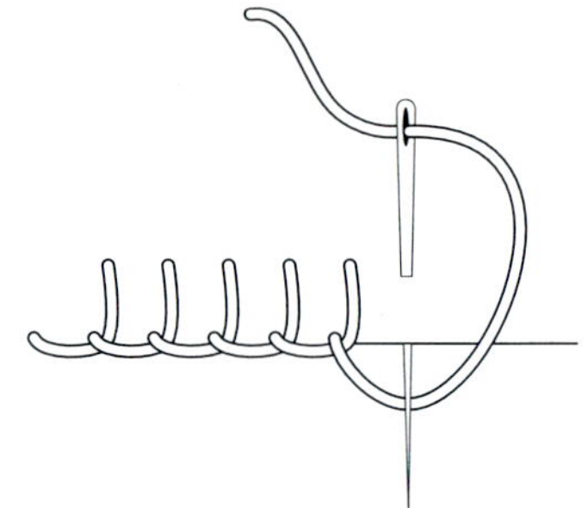

Buttonhole Stitch Diagram

4. Repeat steps 2–3 to make 10 butterfly blocks.

5. Referring to photograph, alternate butterfly blocks with triangle blocks. Join blocks to make 5 horizontal rows of 4 blocks. Join rows to assemble quilt top.

Quilting

Outline-quilt seam lines and butterfly wings.

Finished Edges

Referring to instructions on page 11, make 5 yards of 2½"-wide bias or straight-grain binding from pink. Apply binding to quilt edges.

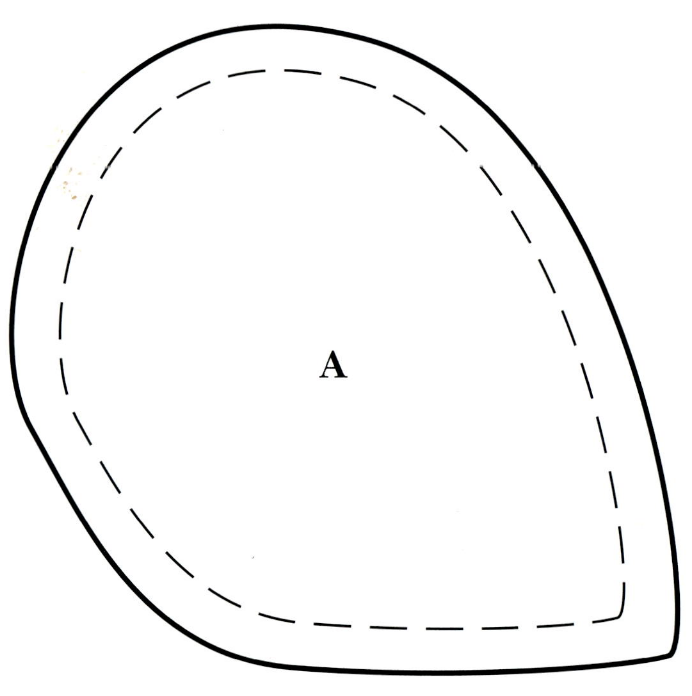

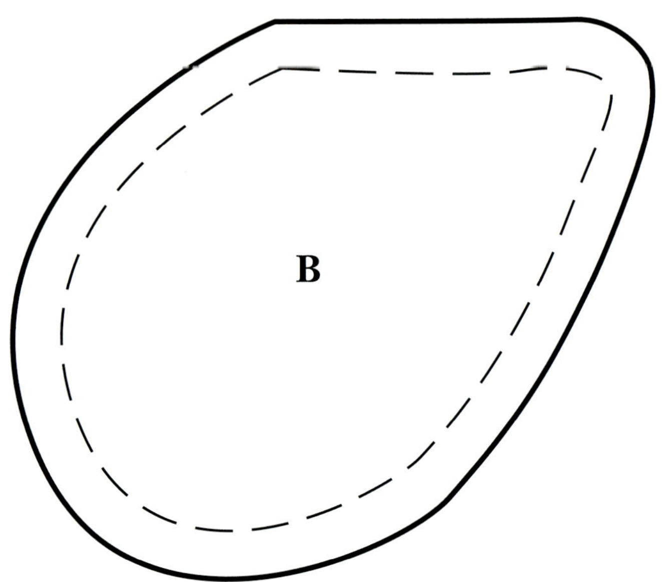

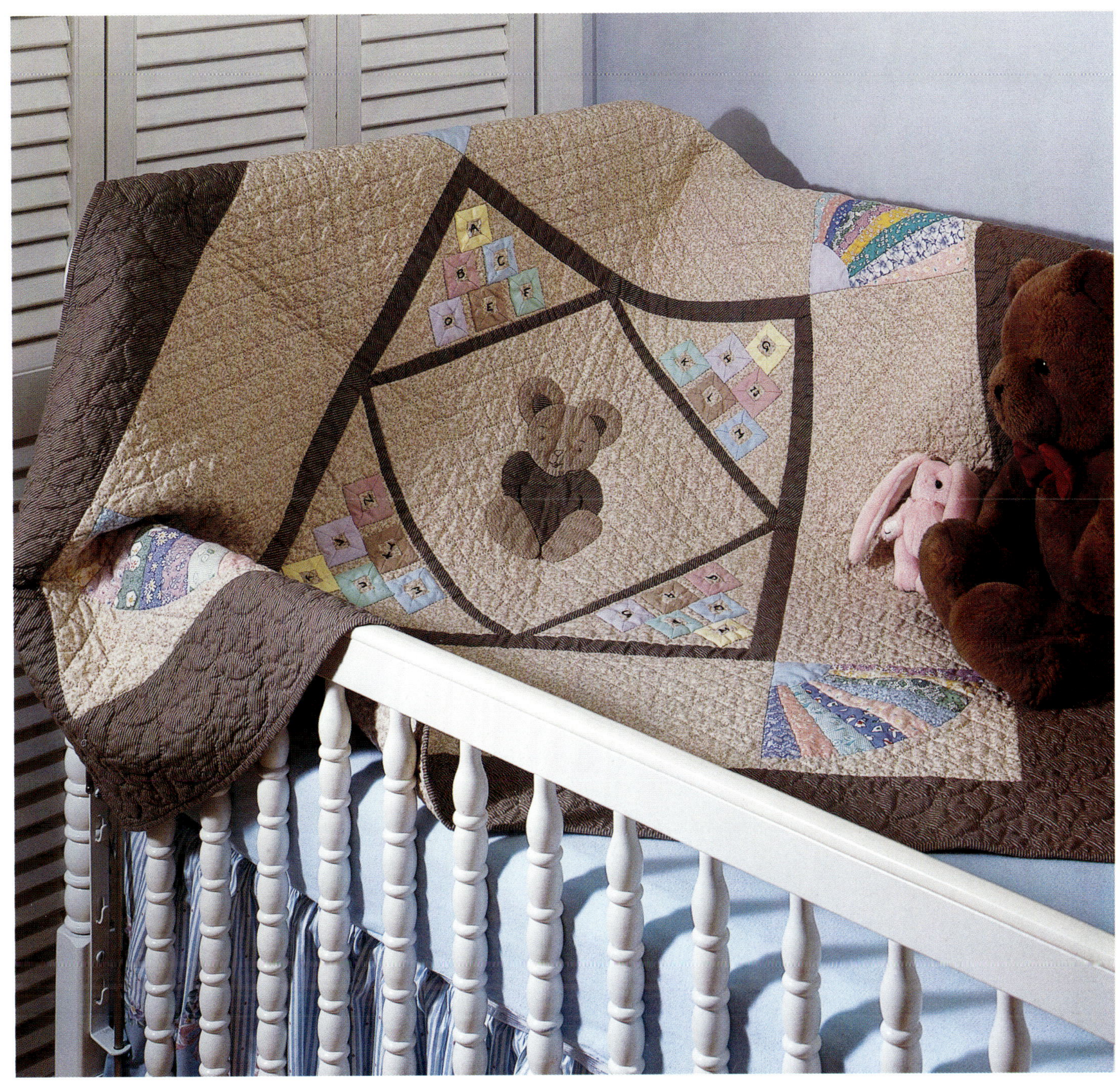

Quilt by Carol Logan Newbill
Homewood, Alabama

Teddy's Fans

Is there a child who isn't a fan of teddy bears? Combine this darling bear, first published in *The Kansas City Star* in 1932, with alphabet blocks and Grandmother's Fan corners to make a delightful quilt for a special little someone.

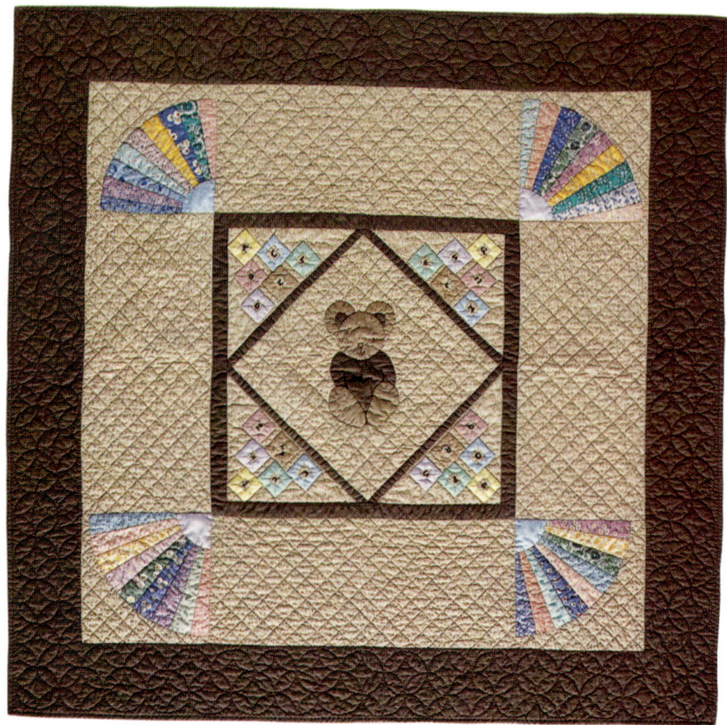

Finished Size

47" x 47"

Fabric Requirements

Dark brown	2¼ yards*
Tan print	1½ yards
Light brown	¼ yard
Assorted prints	1 yard total
Assorted pastels	¾ yard total
Backing	3 yards

*Includes fabric for binding.

Other Materials

Brown embroidery floss

Pieces to Cut**

Template A	4 assorted pastels
Template B	36 assorted prints
Template C	4 tan print
Template D	2 light brown
Template E	2 dark brown
Template F	1 light brown
Template G	1 dark brown
Template H	1 light brown
Template H rev.	1 light brown

**See Step 1 to cut borders and background squares before cutting other pieces.

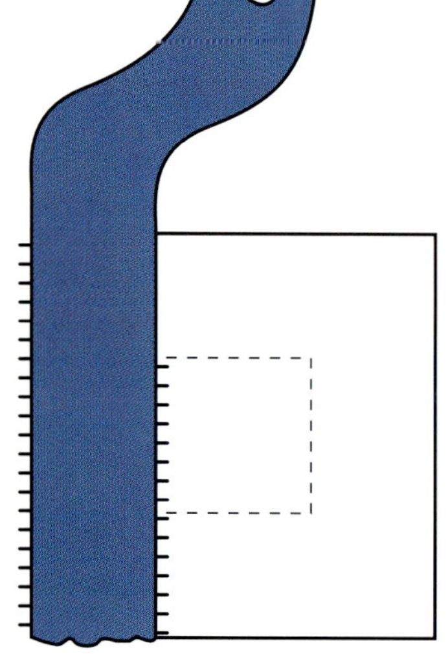

Figure 1

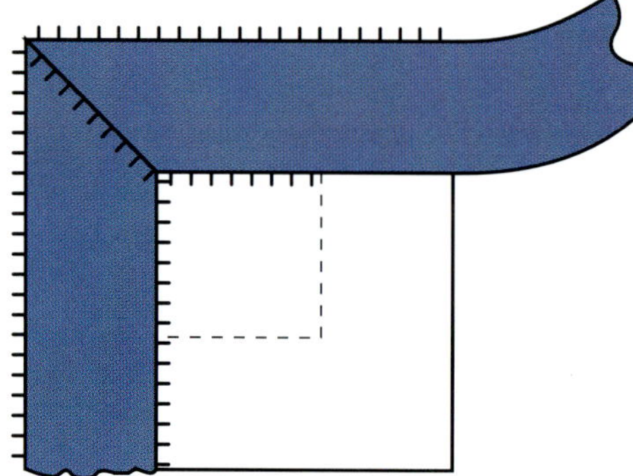

Figure 2

Blocks Appliqué Diagram

Quilt Top Assembly

1. From dark brown, cut 4 (5½" x 47½") strips for outer border, 4 (1½" x 20½") strips for inner border, and 4 (1" x 14") strips for sashing. From tan print, cut 4 (9" x 20½") strips for middle border, 1 (13") square for teddy bear block, and 2 (9⅜") squares. Cut each 9⅜" square in half diagonally to form corner triangles. From assorted pastels, cut 24 (1" x 9") strips for blocks. Set aside.

2. Transfer face markings to F. Using 3 strands of brown floss, satin-stitch eyes, nose, and mouth. Outline-stitch eyebrows and mouth.

3. Referring to **Appliqué Placement Diagram,** appliqué G, Ds, Es, F, H, and H rev. to 13" square. Join sashing strips to square, mitering corners.

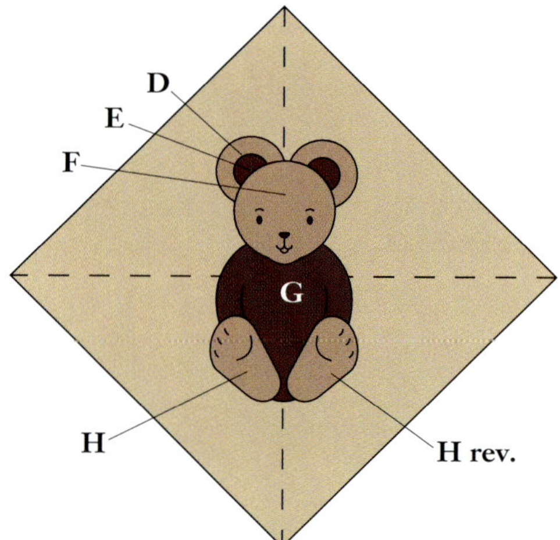

Appliqué Placement Diagram

4. Fold under ¼" on each long edge of 1 pastel strip; press. Repeat for remaining strips.

Transfer Blocks Appliqué Guidelines to 4 corner triangles. Aligning short edge of 1 strip with bottom of 1 block guideline, appliqué strip to triangle as shown in **Blocks Appliqué Diagram, Figure 1,** stopping at corners of guidelines. Referring to **Figure 2,** fold and align strip along guidelines; pin. Tuck excess strip neatly into corner, forming miter. Slipstitch miter closed. Appliqué remaining sides of block in same manner. Repeat to appliqué remaining blocks, varying colors as shown in photograph.

5. Using 3 strands of brown floss and referring to photograph, embroider 1 letter of alphabet in each block, placing "I J" in 1 block and "X Y" in 1 block.

Join triangles to corners of bear block to form center medallion. Join inner border strips to center medallion. See page 8 for instructions on mitering corners.

6. Referring to **Fan Block Assembly Diagram,** join 1 A, 9 Bs, and 1 C to form 1 Fan block. Repeat to make 4 Fan blocks.

7. Join 1 Fan block to each end of 1 middle border strip to make top border. Repeat to make bottom border. Join remaining 2 middle border strips to sides of quilt. Join top and bottom borders to quilt.

8. Join outer borders to quilt, mitering corners.

Quilting

Outline-quilt bear, blocks, and fans. Quilt 1" crosshatch pattern across background of quilt. Quilt borders as desired.

Finished Edges

Referring to instructions on page 11, make 5¼ yards of 2½"-wide bias or straight-grain binding from dark brown. Apply binding to quilt edges.

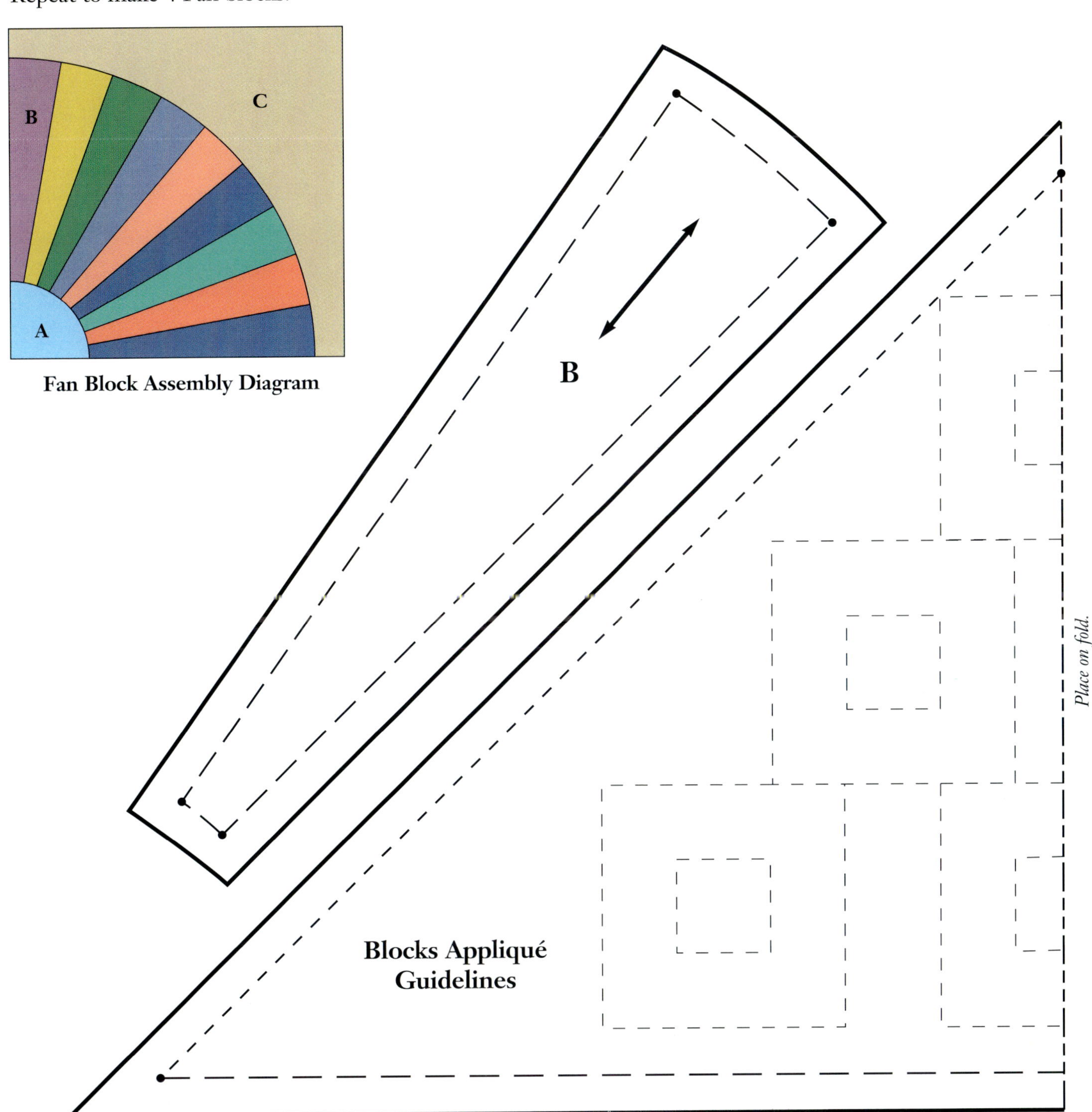

Fan Block Assembly Diagram

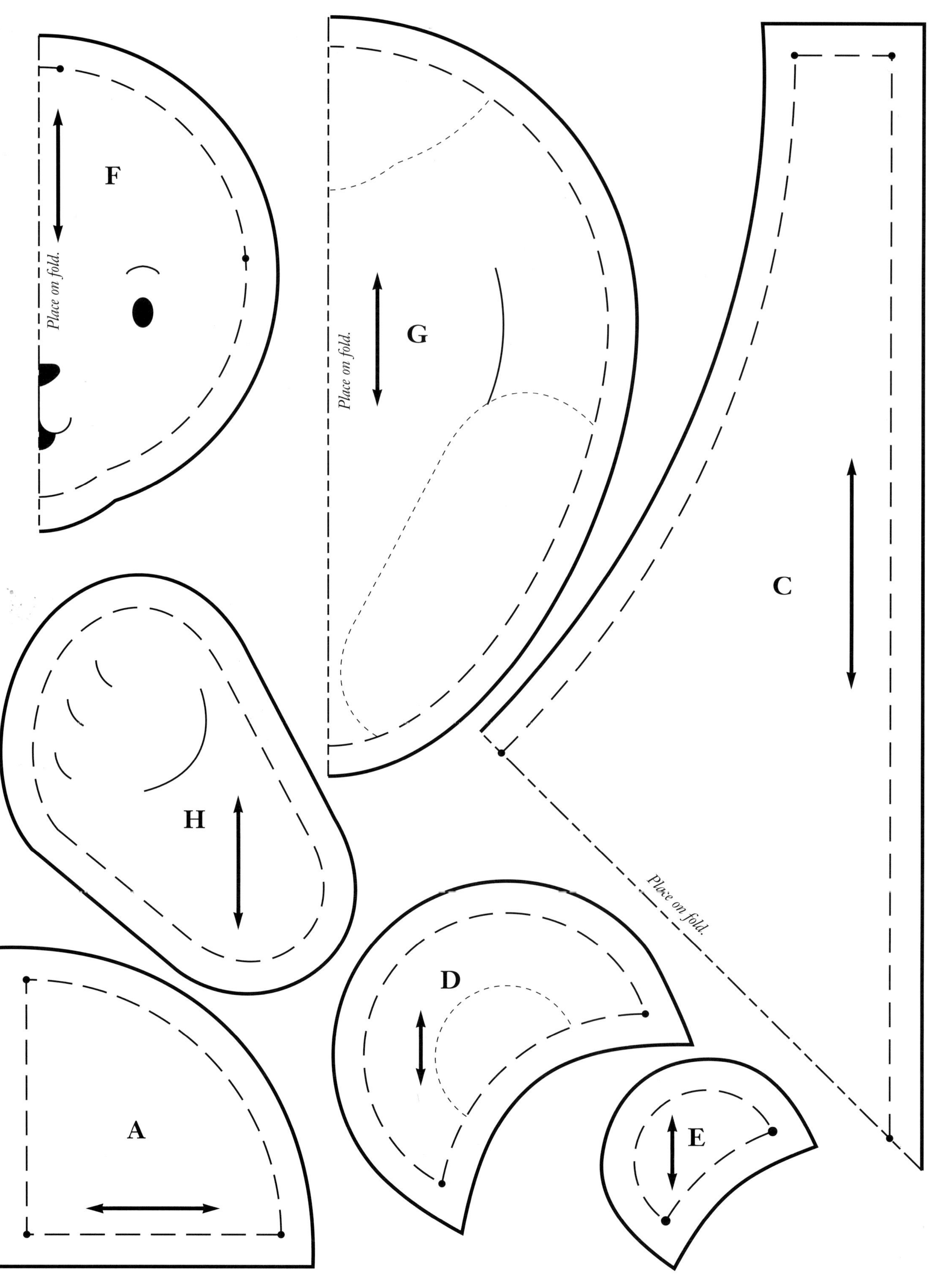
F
Place on fold.
G
Place on fold.
C
H
Place on fold.
D
A
E

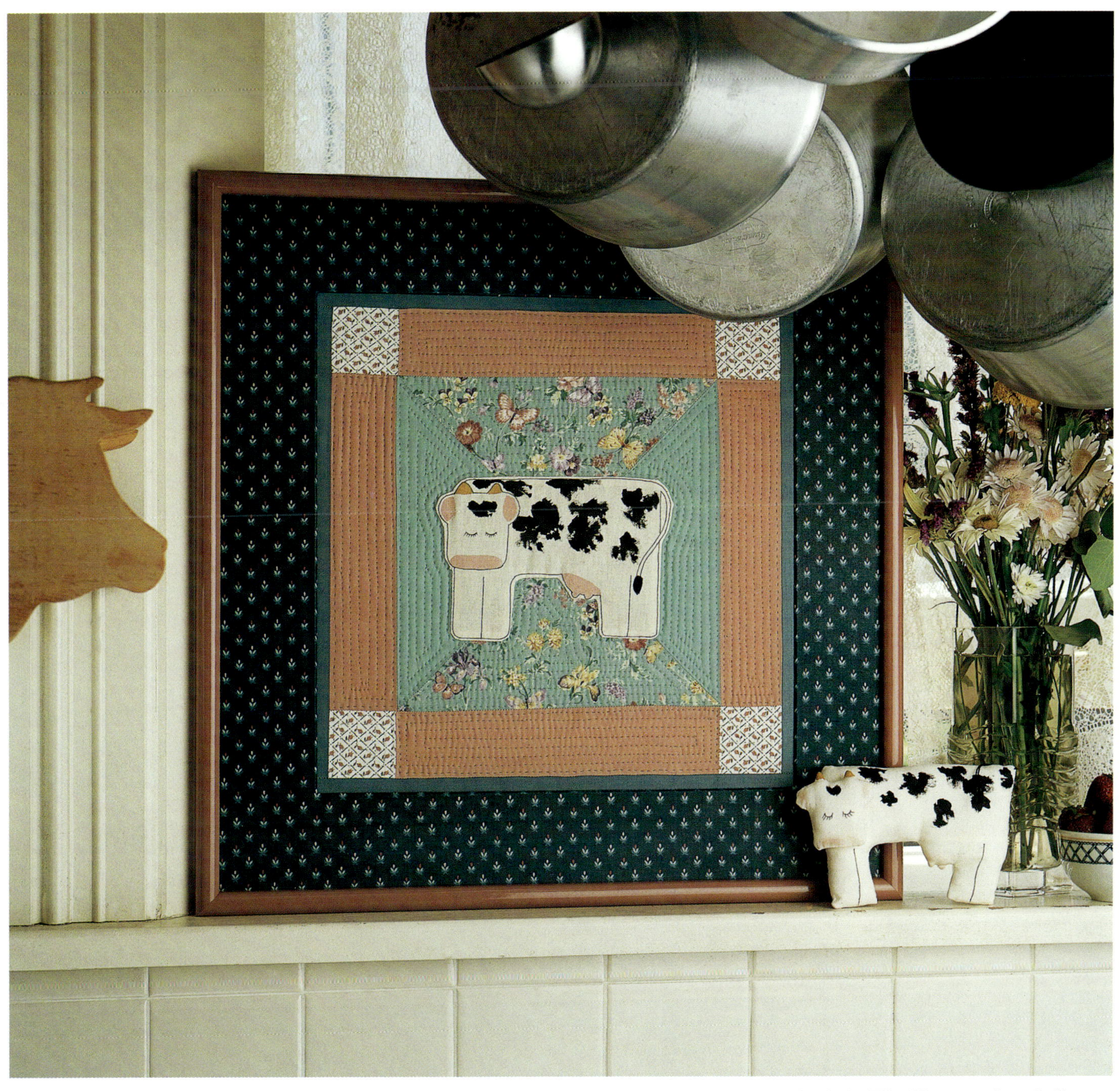

Quilt by The Vanessa-Ann Collection
Ogden, Utah

Cow in the Clover

Make this charming country quilt in a weekend. Or use the cow pattern by itself and stitch an ornament for country decorating or gift giving.

Finished Size
16½" x 16½"

Fabric Requirements

Muslin	⅝ yard
Green	12" square
Green print	12" square
Pink	⅛ yard
Cream/pink print	scrap
Blue-green	¼ yard

Pieces to Cut*

Template A	2 green 2 green print
Template B	4 cream/pink print
Template C	1 muslin

*See Step 4 before cutting Template C.

Other Materials
Fabric paints: gold, pink, black
Paintbrush
Fine-tip permanent black marker
Green quilting thread
Wooden frame
Fabric-covered mat board

Quilt Top Assembly

1. Referring to **Block Assembly Diagram,** join 1 green A to 1 green print A. Repeat to make 2 pieced triangles. Join pieced triangles to make center square as shown.

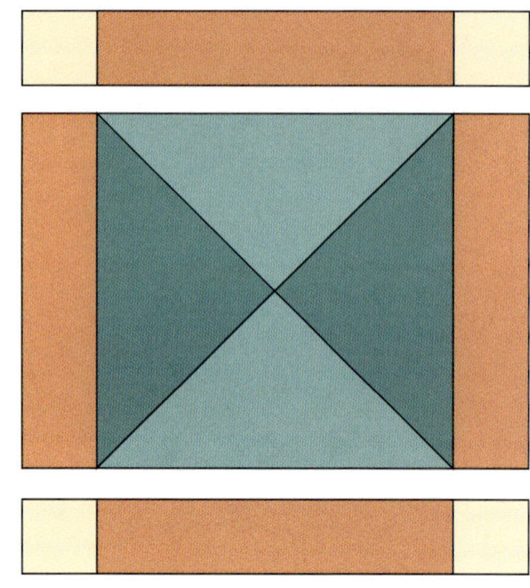

Block Assembly Diagram

2. From pink, cut 4 (2½" x 10") sashing strips. Referring to **Block Assembly Diagram,** join 1 sashing strip to each side of center square. Join 1 B to each end of remaining sashing strips. Join pieced strips to top and bottom of center square.

3. From blue-green, cut 4 (1½" x 16½") strips for border. Join border strips to sides of quilt. Join remaining border strips to top and bottom of quilt.

4. Trace Template C onto muslin, but do not cut out. Referring to photograph and pattern, paint spots black, horns gold,

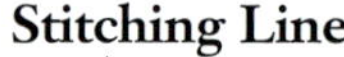

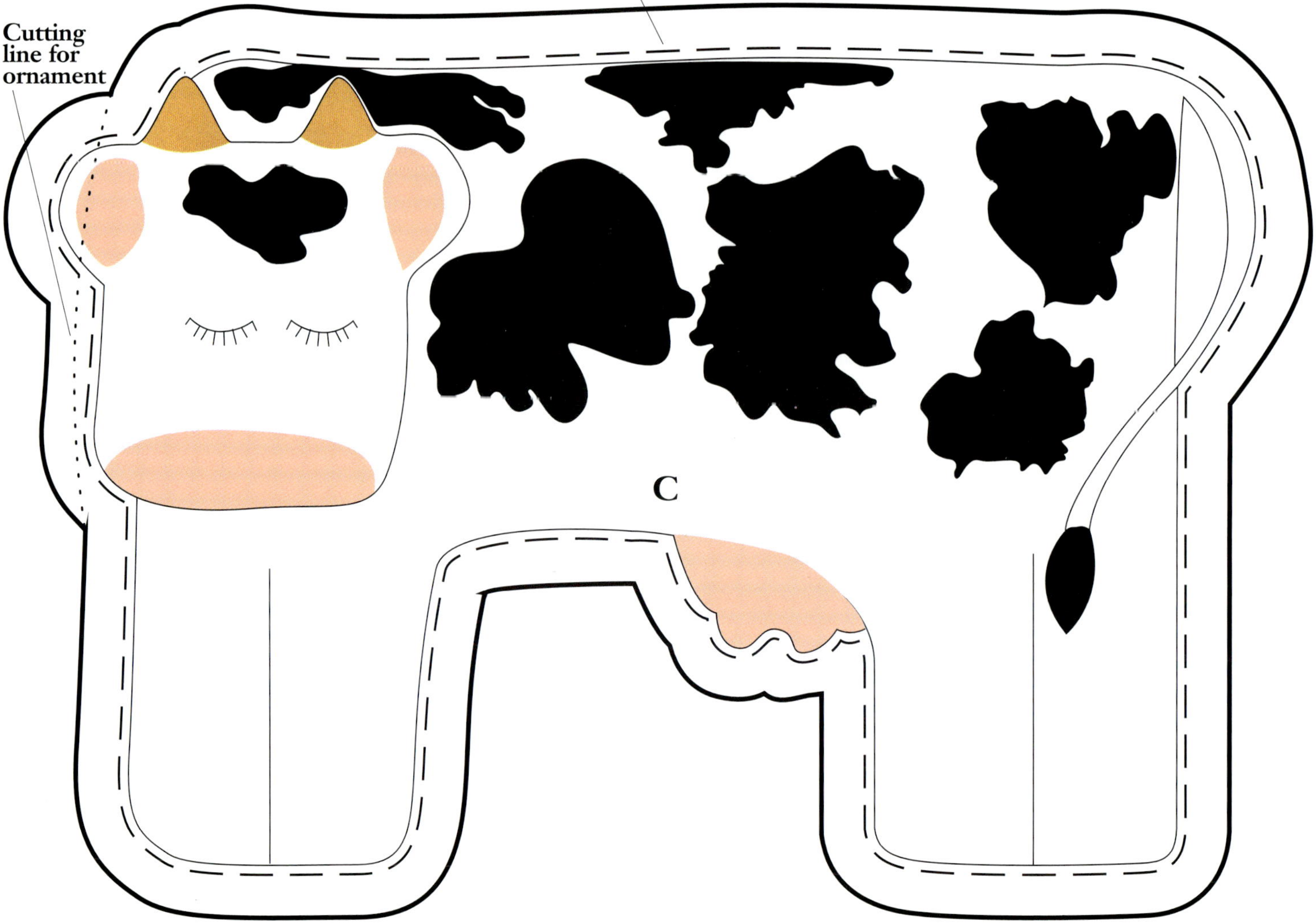

Cutting line for ornament

C

and ears, muzzle, and udder pink. Using black pen, outline cow and draw eyelashes. Cut out cow. Referring to **Appliqué Placement Diagram**, center cow on quilt and appliqué.

Quilting

Echo-quilt cow, sashing strips, and corners.

Finished Edges

Mat and frame quilt as desired.

A Quick Country Cow

To make cow ornament in photograph, transfer body pattern to muslin, omitting head, and cut 2. Paint front piece as described in Step 4 of Quilt Top Assembly, but do not outline cow. Referring to pattern, outline legs and tail.

With right sides facing and all edges aligned, join body pieces, leaving open at bottom. Turn and stuff. Slipstitch opening closed. Repeat to make cow head, adding ¼" seam allowance when cutting. Referring to photograph for placement, sew back of head to front of body.

If desired, stitch a length of thread through center top of ornament and knot ends together for hanger loop.

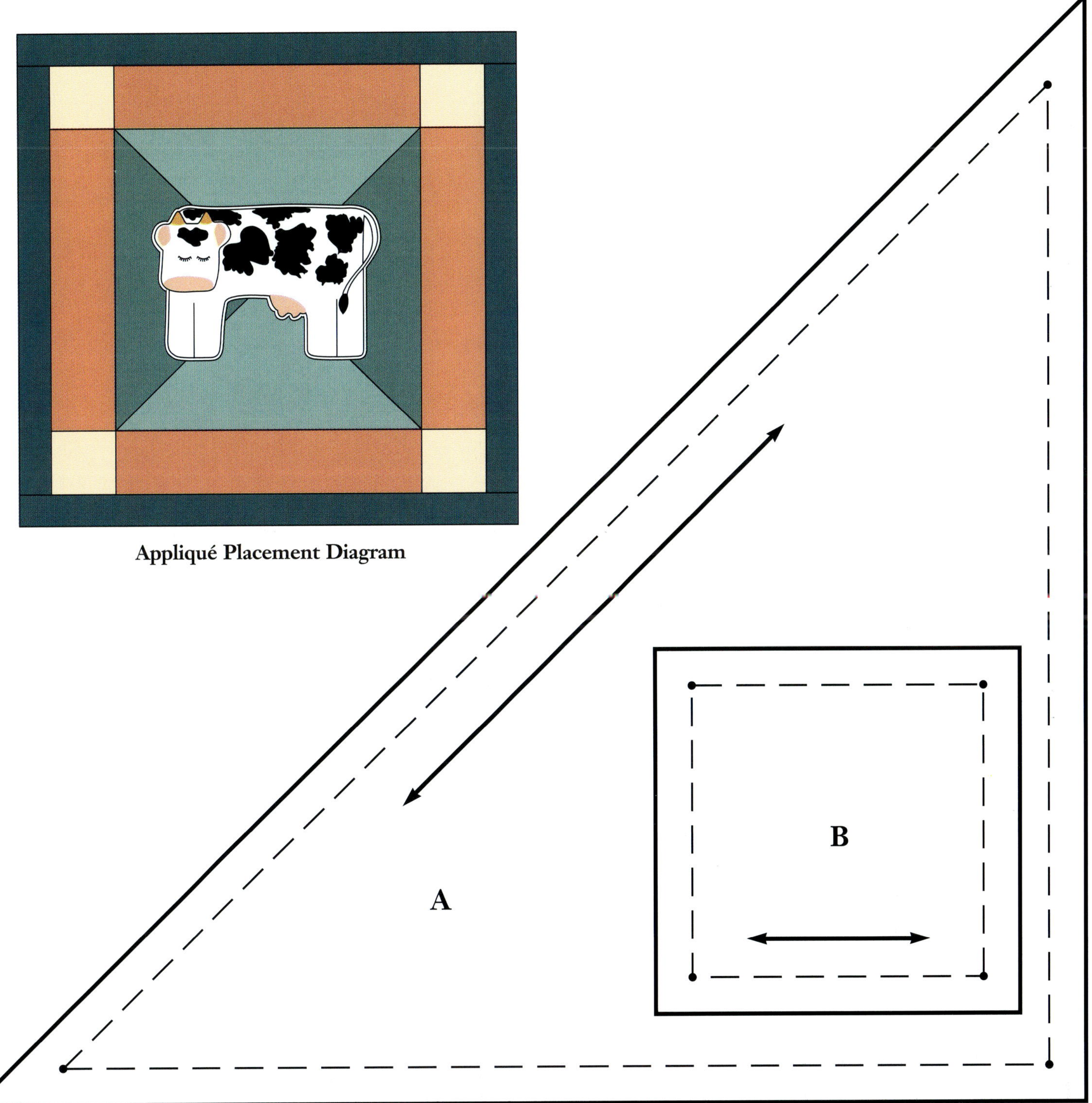

Appliqué Placement Diagram

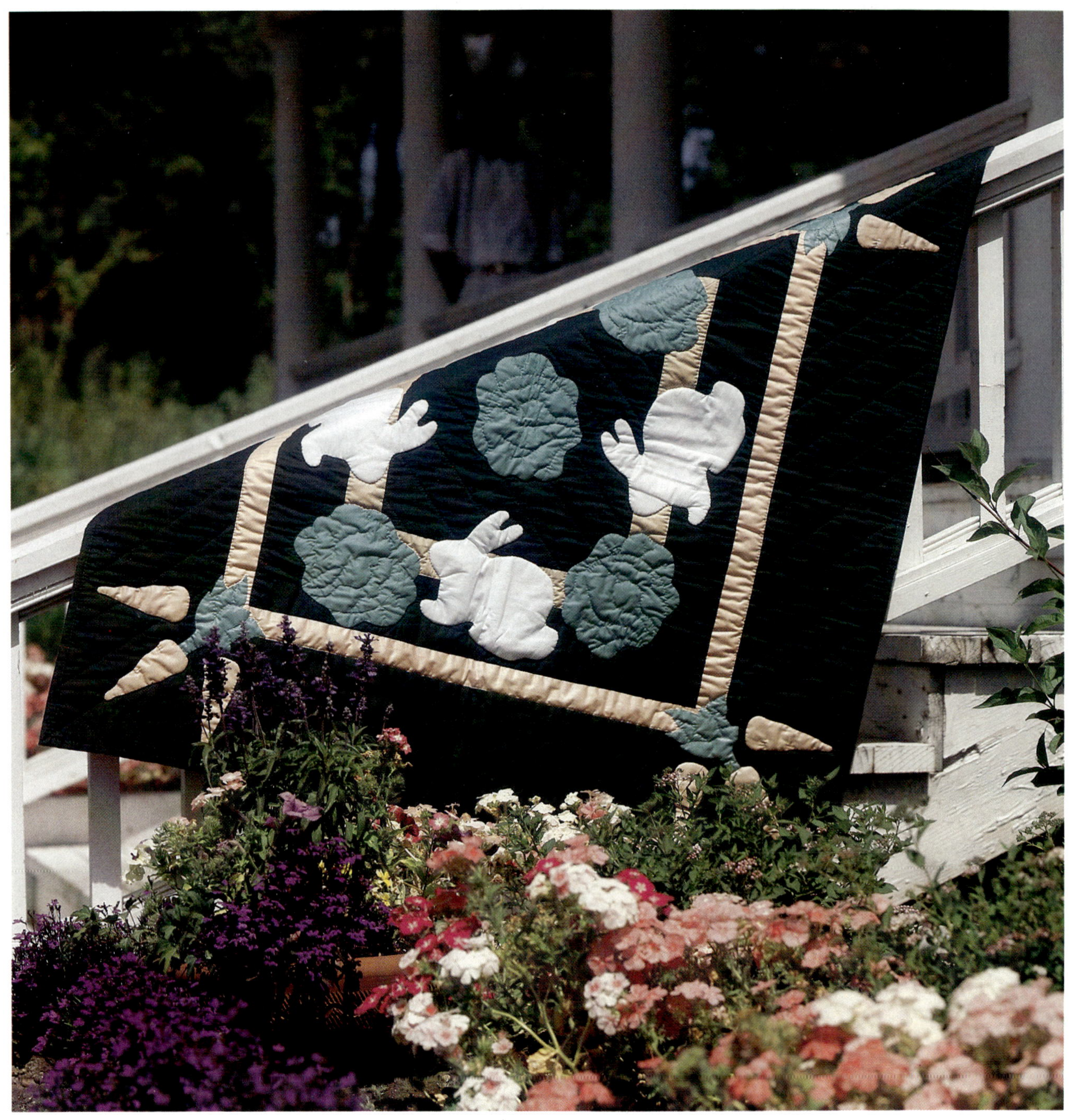

Bunnies in the Garden

Bunnies can nibble to their hearts' content in this appliquéd garden. Sweet carrots and lush cabbages await them at every corner. The large, simple shapes make this a great quilt for beginners.

Finished Quilt Size

46" x 46"

Fabric Requirements

Dark green	3¾ yards*
Light green	⅝ yard
Apricot	1⅜ yard
White	¼ yard
Tan	⅜ yard

*Includes fabric for backing.

Other Materials

Additional ¼ yard batting
Light green quilting thread

Number to Cut

Template A	4 white 4 batting**
Template B	12 apricot
Template C	4 light green
Template D	4 light green
Template E	4 light green
Template F	5 light green
Template G	5 light green
Template H	5 light green
Template I	5 light green

**Cut batting without seam allowance.

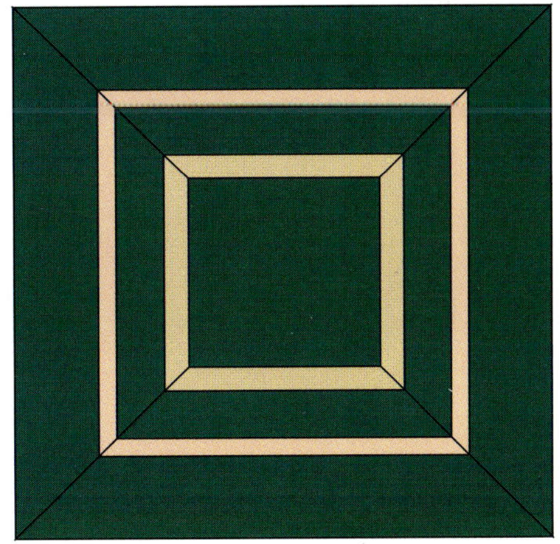

Assembly Diagram

Quilt Top Assembly

1. From dark green, cut a 16½" square for center. Also from dark green, cut 4 (7½" x 48") strips and 4 (4½" x 30") strips. From apricot, cut 4 (2" x 48") strips. From tan, cut 4 (2½" x 30") strips.

2. To assemble border, center and join 1 (7½" x 48") dark green strip to 1 apricot strip along 1 long edge. Then center and join 1 (4½" x 30") dark green strip to remaining long edge of apricot strip. Center and join 1 tan strip to remaining long edge of (4½" x 30") dark green strip. Repeat process to make 4 borders.

3. Mark centers on tan edge of each border. Mark centers on edges of center square. Referring to **Assembly Diagram** and matching center of border and center square, join 1 border strip to each edge. See page 8 for instructions on mitering border corners.

4. Center and pin 1 white A on 1 batting A. Referring to **Appliqué Placement Diagram, Figure 1,** appliqué bunny to quilt. Repeat to appliqué remaining bunnies.

5. Appliqué Bs, Cs, Ds, and Es to quilt, referring to **Appliqué Placement Diagram, Figure 2,** for order of placement. Appliqué Fs, Gs, Hs, and Is to quilt, referring to **Figure 3** for order of placement.

6. From dark green, piece a 48" square for backing.

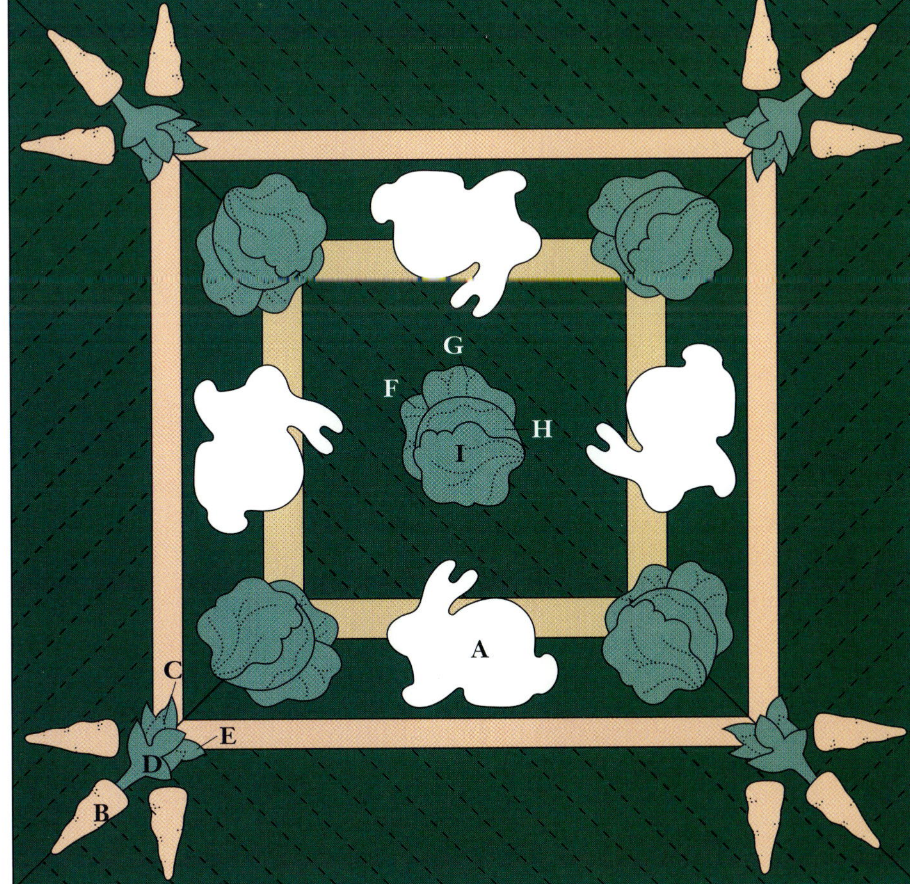

Appliqué Placement Diagram–Figure 1

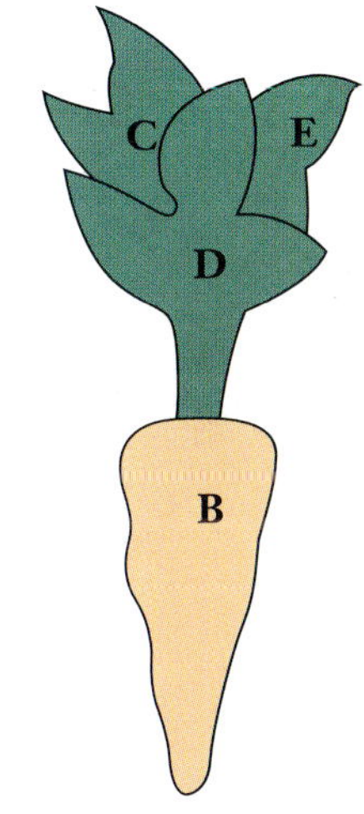

Figure 2

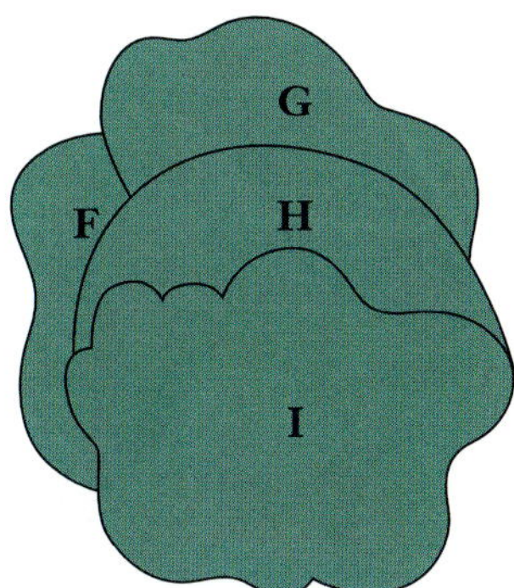

Figure 3

Quilting

Outline-quilt appliqués. Quilt details on carrots and cabbages. Quilt diagonal lines in quilt center and outer dark green border.

Finished Edges

Fold backing to quilt front along each edge. Turn under ½" and slipstitch to front, mitering corners.

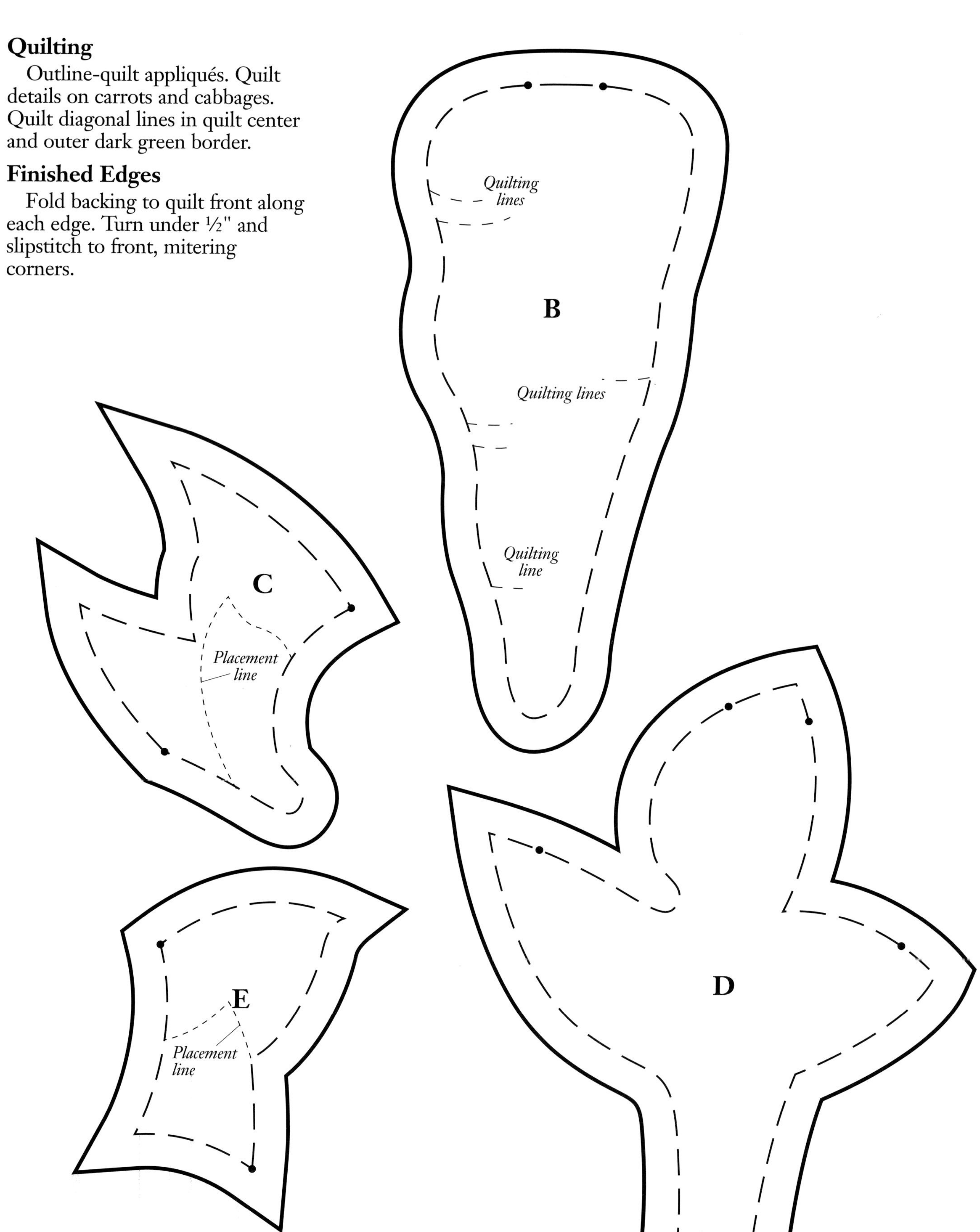

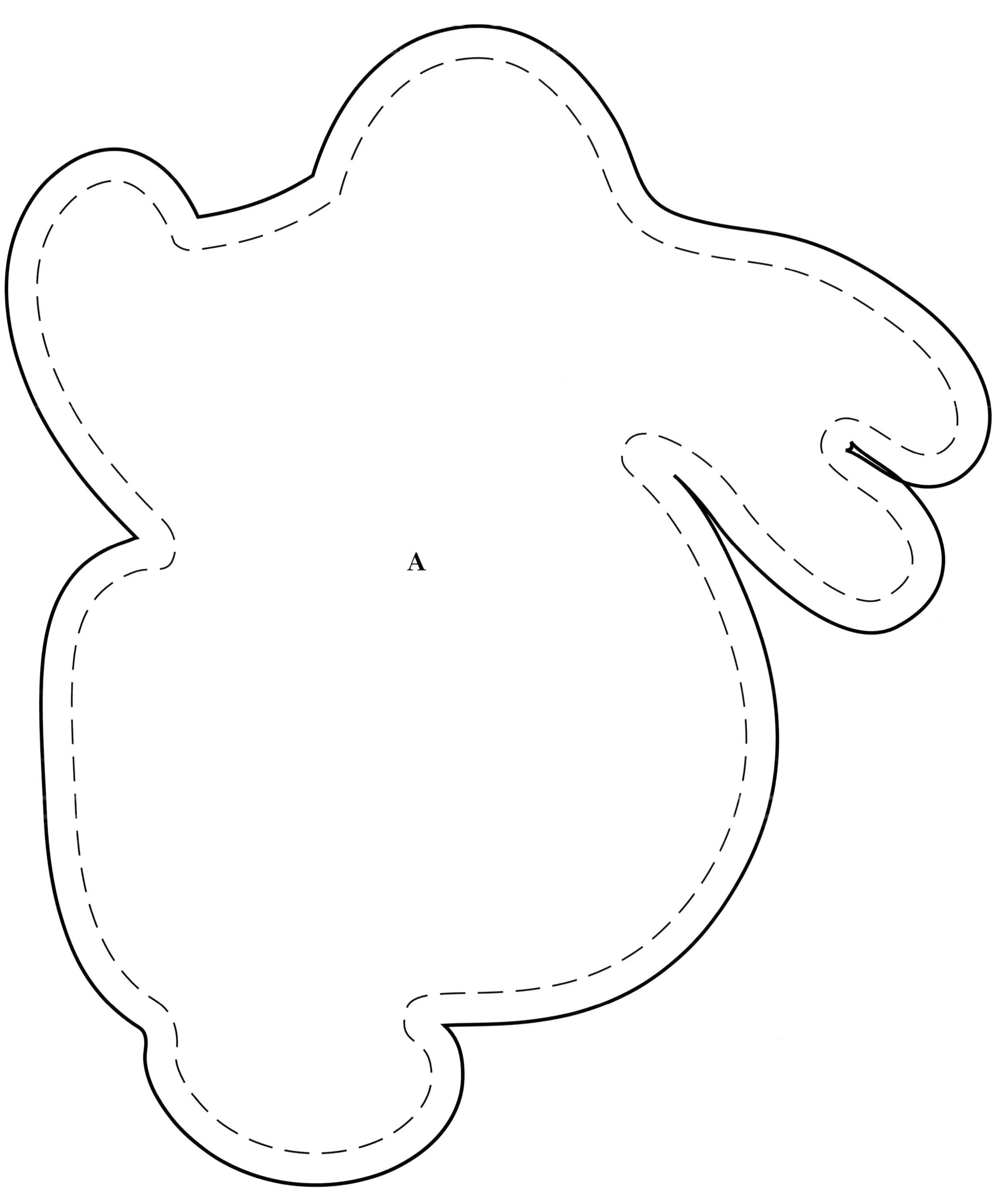
A

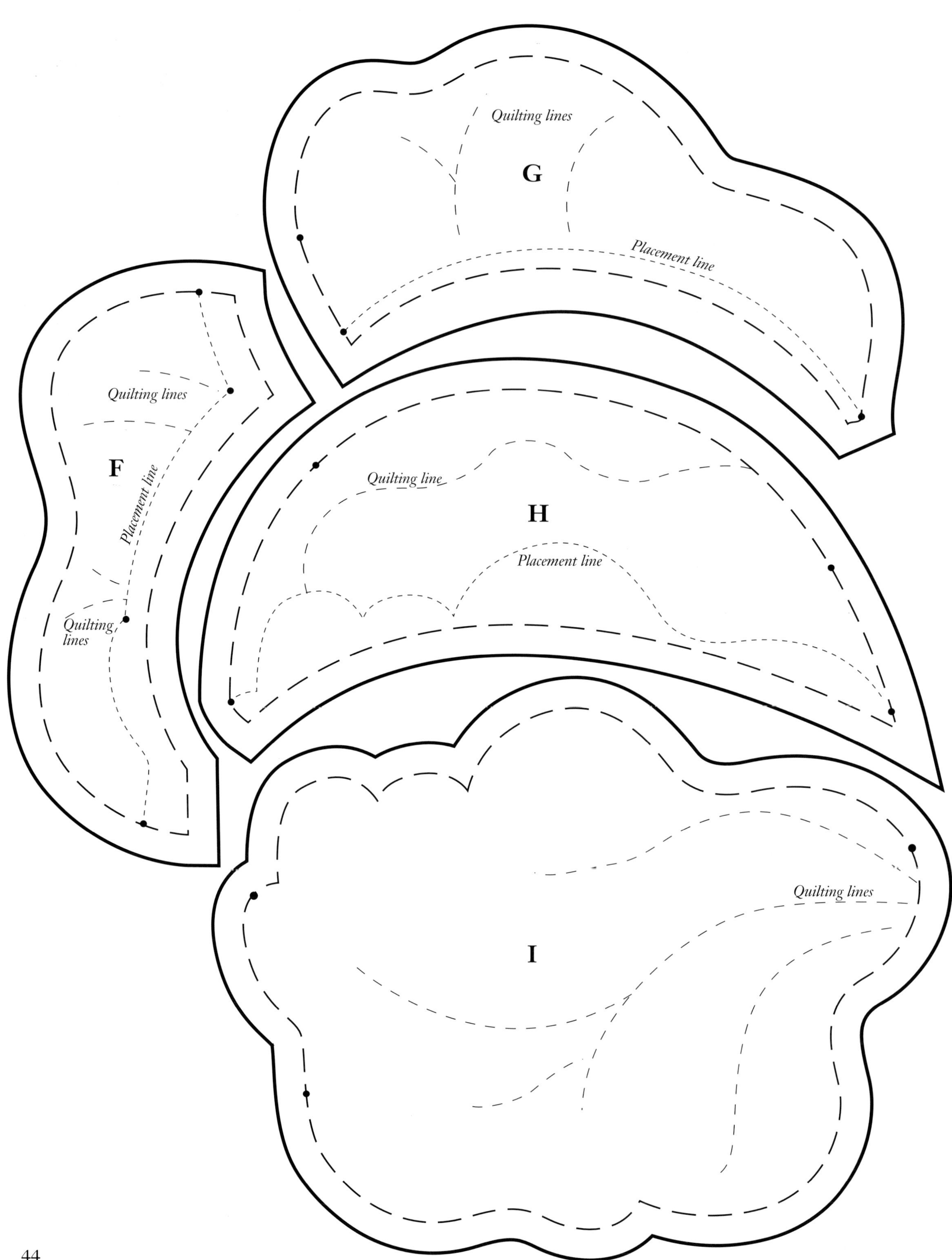
Quilting lines
G
Placement line
Quilting lines
F
Placement line
Quilting lines
Quilting line
H
Placement line
Quilting lines
I

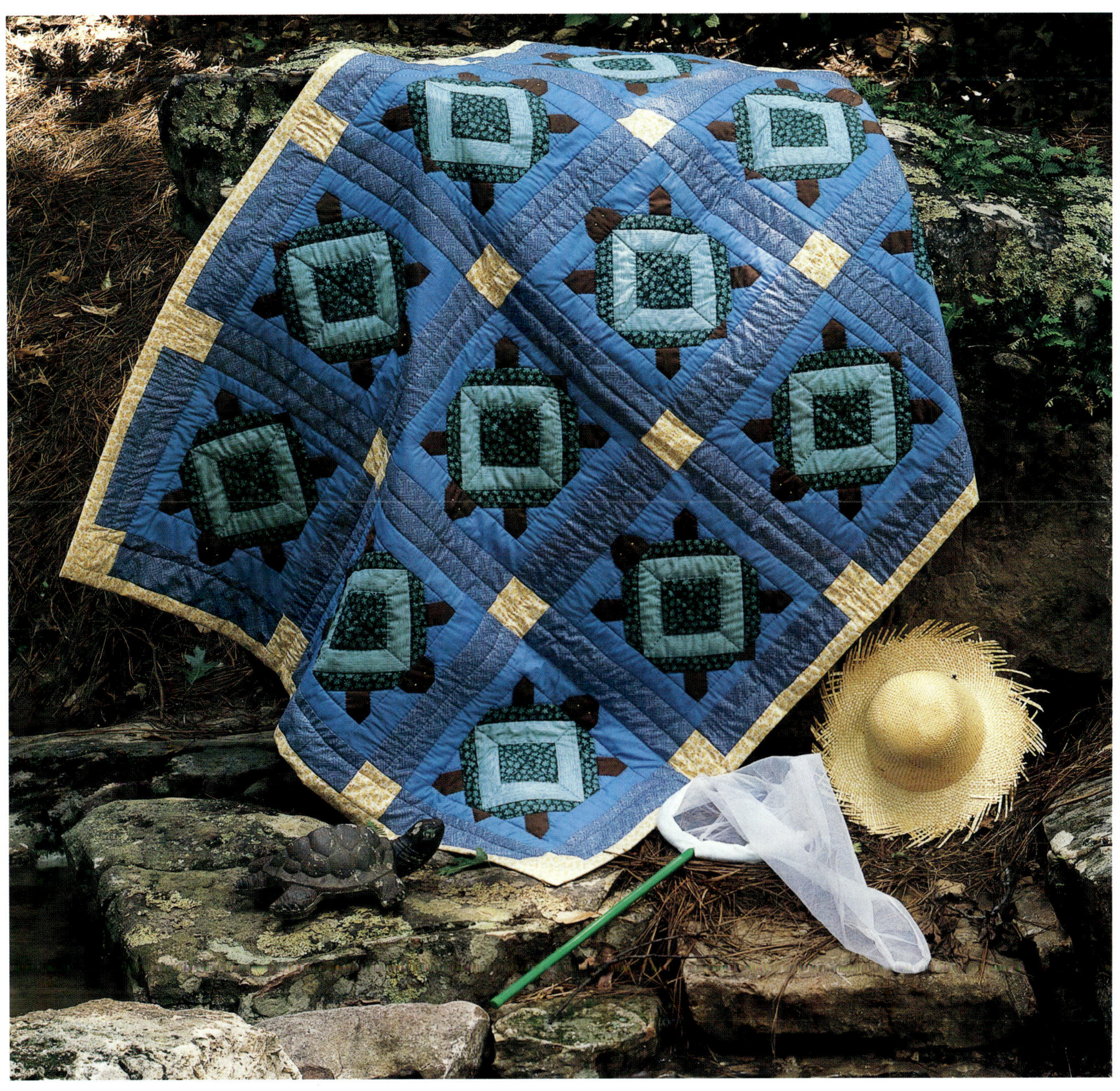

Quilt designed by Susan Ramey Cleveland
Leeds, Alabama
Made by Carol Tipton
Calera, Alabama

Turtle Creek

These box turtles are a creekside favorite at picnics and outings. Using strip-pieced shells and simple sashing, you'll be surprised by the speed of the assembly.

Finished Quilt Size
48" x 63"

Number of Blocks and Finished Size
12 blocks 12" x 12"

Fabric Requirements

Blue print	1¼ yards
Blue	1 yard
Dark green print	1¼ yards
Yellow print	¾ yard*
Light green print	½ yard
Brown	½ yard
Backing	3 yards

*Includes fabric for binding.

Other Materials
Yellow embroidery floss

Number to Cut**

Template A	12 brown
Template B	24 blue
Template D	12 brown
	96 blue
Template E	48 brown
Template H	12 blue
Template H rev.	12 blue

**See Step 1 to cut C, G, and sashing before cutting other pieces.

Quilt Top Assembly

1. For C, cut 2 (5¼" x 42") strips from blue. Cut strips into 24 (2½" x 5¼") rectangles. For G, cut 6 (2" x 42") strips from blue. Cut strips into 24 (2" x 9½") rectangles. Set Cs and Gs aside.

Cut 11 (3½" x 42") strips from blue print. Cut strips into 31 (3½" x 12½") sashing strips. From yellow print, cut 20 (3½") sashing squares. Set aside.

2. To make Top Section, join 1 B to each diagonal edge of 1 A, referring to **Block Assembly Diagram.** Join 1 C to each side of A/B unit. Repeat to make 12 Top Sections. Set aside.

3. Join 1 blue D to each side of 1 E. Repeat to make 48 D/E/D units. Set aside.

4. From light green print, cut 7 (1⅞" x 43") strips. From dark green print, cut 14 (2⅜" x 43") strips. Join 1 dark green strip to each long edge of 1 light green strip. Repeat to make 7 strip units.

Mark seam placement lines on Template F. Referring to **Cutting Diagram,** position Template F on 1 strip unit, aligning seam placement lines with seam lines and top point of template with top edge of strip unit. Mark and cut 1 F. Turn template, aligning top point of template with bottom edge of strip unit and diagonal edge of template with cut end of strip unit. Mark and cut 1 F. Repeat process to cut 48 Fs.

5. Referring to **Block Assembly Diagram,** join 1 F to 1 D/E/D unit. Join 4 D/E/D/F units to make middle unit. Join 1 G to each side of middle unit to make Middle Section. Repeat to make 12 Middle Sections. Set aside.

6. Join 1 H and 1 H rev. to 1 brown D to make Bottom Section. Repeat to make 12 Bottom Sections.

7. Referring to **Block Assembly Diagram,** join sections to make 12 turtle blocks. Using 3 strands of embroidery floss, make French knots for turtles' eyes.

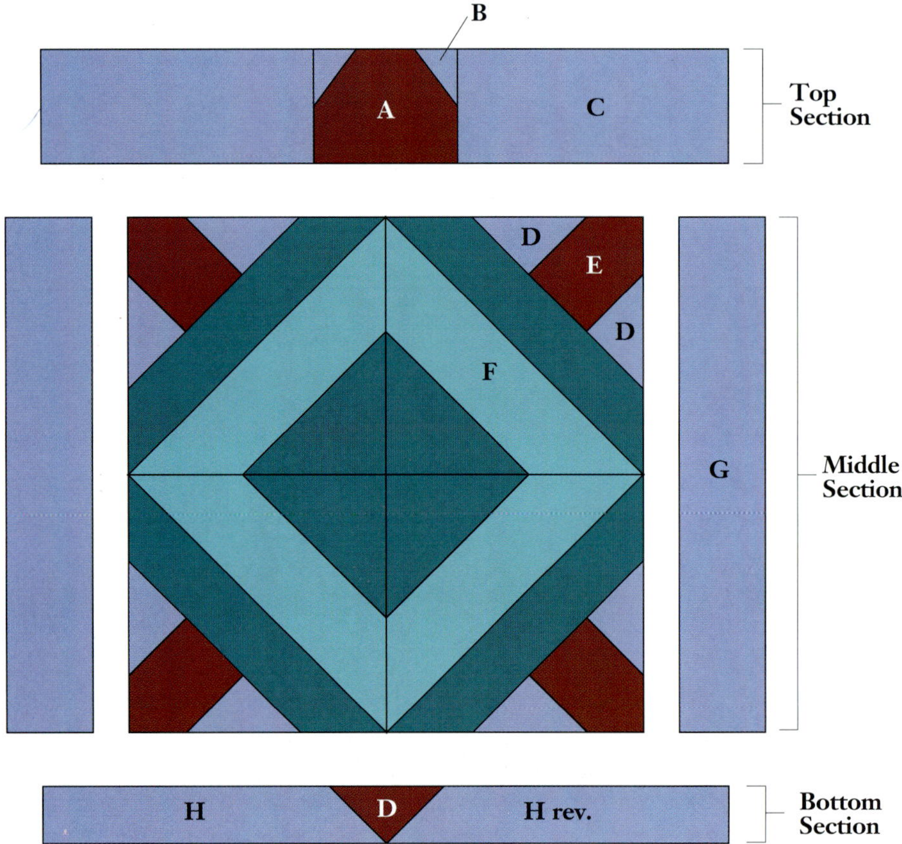

Block Assembly Diagram

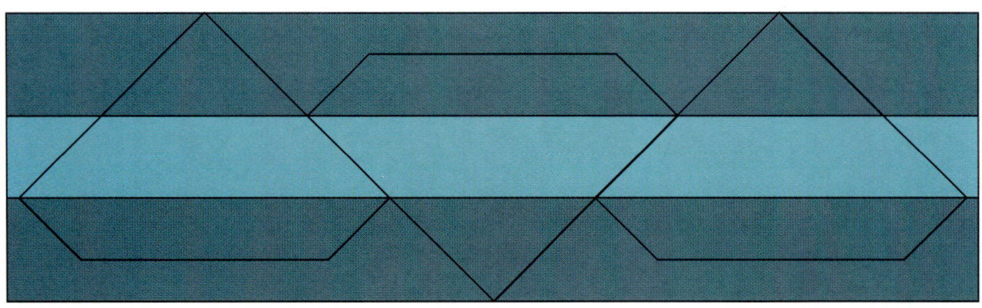

Cutting Diagram

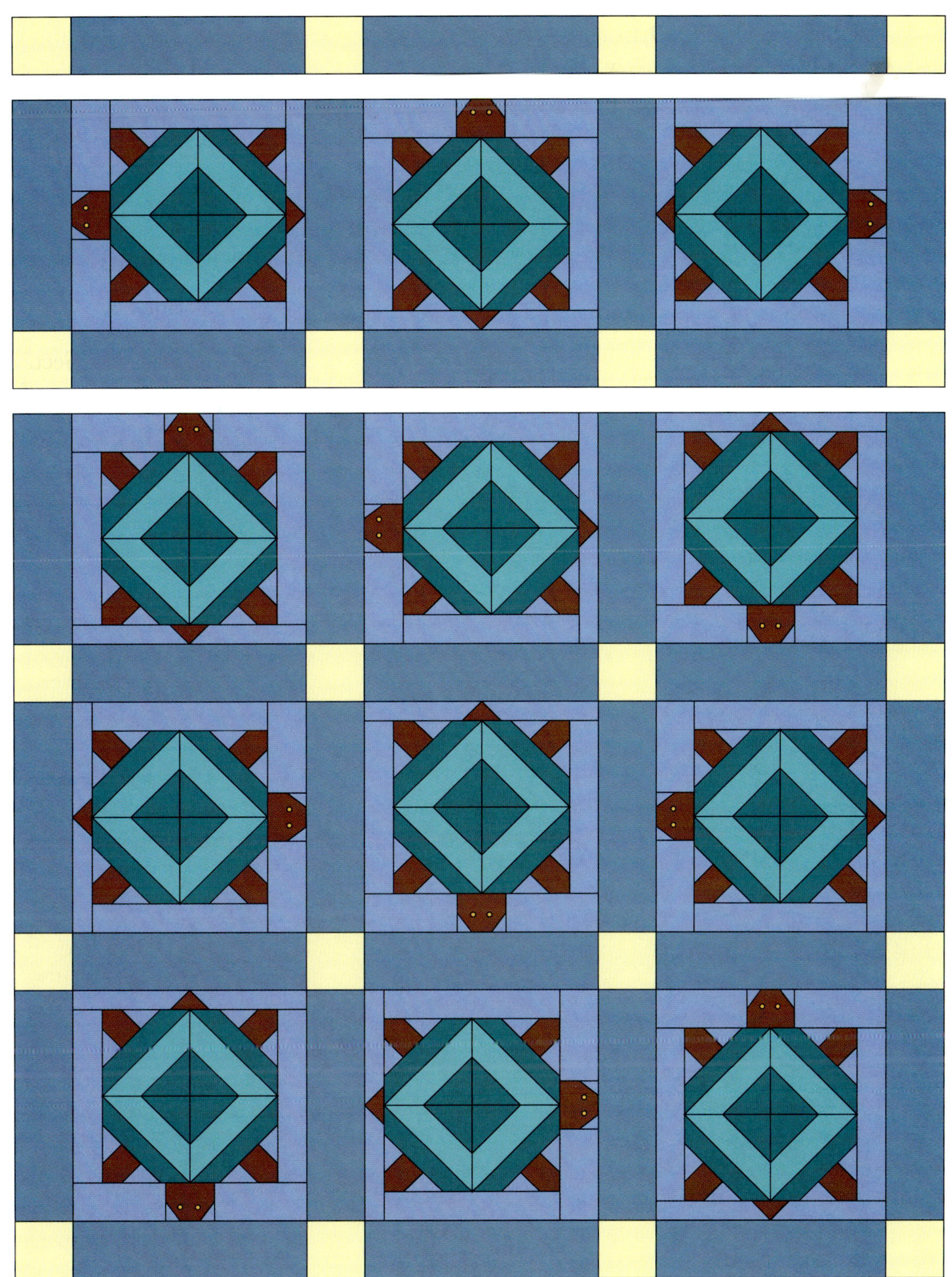

Setting Diagram

8. Beginning and ending with a sashing square, alternate 4 sashing squares with 3 sashing strips. Join to make 1 sashing row. Repeat to make 5 sashing rows.

9. Referring to **Setting Diagram** for direction of turtles, alternate 4 sashing strips with 3 blocks and join. Repeat to make 4 horizontal rows. Join rows, alternating sashing rows with block rows.

Quilting

Outline-quilt patchwork. Quilt sashing as desired.

Finishing

Referring to instructions on page 11, make 5 yards of 2½"-wide bias or straight-grain binding from yellow print. Apply binding to quilt edges.

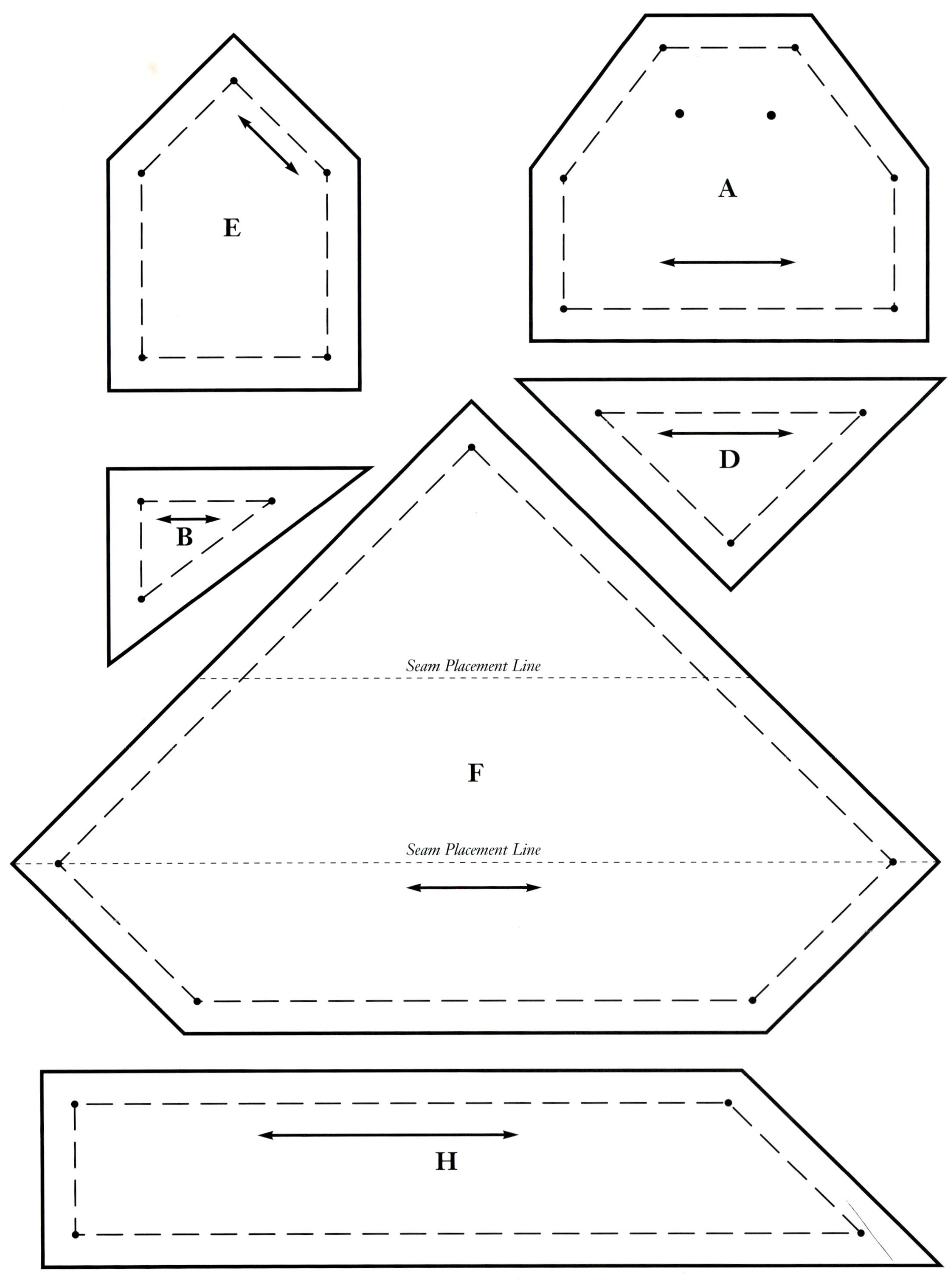
E
A
D
B
Seam Placement Line
F
Seam Placement Line
H